D1002771

PRISM OF VALUE

CONNECT, CONVINCE AND INFLUENCE WHEN IT MATTERS MOST

by

Liz Wainger

TELEMACHUS PRESS

PRISM OF VALUE: CONNECT, CONVINCE AND INFLUENCE WHEN IT MATTERS MOST

Cover designed by Arrowdesigns

Published by Telemachus Press, LLC
7652 Sawmill Road
Suite 304
Dublin, Ohio 43016
http://www.telemachuspress.com

Visit the author website:
http://www.waingergroup.com

ISBN: 978-1-948046-23-7 (eBook)
ISBN: 978-1-948046-24-4 (Paperback)

Library of Congress Location Number: 2018954867

Version 2018.08.28

This book is dedicated to my brother David Lazarus.

Table of Contents

Acknowledgments

I am deeply grateful to my family, friends and colleagues without whom this book would never have been written. To my brother Dave, whose safe deposit box was the inspiration for the book. To my husband Bill and daughters Natalie and Julia for their love and continual encouragement to stop talking and start writing the book I had been promising to write for more than a decade. To my good friend and colleague Jan Johnson for her many reads, late night conversations, unwavering support for this book and so many other endeavors. To Orvel Ray Wilson and Martha Finney, wonderful editors and coaches, who helped me get this book out of my head and who constructively challenged me to make it better. To Louise Boulton-Lear who offered sage advice. To Arrowdesigns for creating a beautiful book cover. To Greg Johnson and Carol Ochs, whose eagle eyes caught typos and other errors. To my clients, who have taught me so much about communication, team work and bouncing back from adversity.

Introduction

On a cool summer morning in Chamonix, France, I looked up at Mont Blanc, one of the tallest mountains in Europe. My family and I had arrived the night before in the dark, so I was looking forward to seeing the mountain with the first light. But as I stepped outside the quaint house we had rented, all I could see were trees shrouded in milky mist. A few days later, when the sun came out, I could finally see the snowcapped peak, the glaciers running down the mountain and its sheer mass. It was spectacular. Beauty and majesty revealed.

Had the sun never emerged, I would never have truly appreciated Mont Blanc. This experience made me think of how too many of us shroud ourselves in metaphorical clouds of fog that prevent our bosses, would-be clients, partners, and even our own teams from seeing our value.

This book is designed to help you *be understood*. In our personal and business lives, we can't move forward without other people. When our bosses, clients and customers don't *get* us, we get left behind. You don't get the job or promotion you want. Your competitor lands the big client you've chased for a year. Your business idles, stuck on stagnant.

You do good work and you're working hard, but chances are you are leaving your value and your opportunity to succeed on the table. You haven't figured out how to tell the people who matter most why you matter. At best you confuse; at worst you bore. Either way, they're tuning out, shifting their attention to someone else.

When I was growing up, I wanted to be an interpreter at the United Nations. Sure, it was glamorous to sit in the glass booth and translate for world leaders, but it was the idea of getting people to understand each other that was compelling. Instead, I became a professional communicator, first as a journalist, then directing PR and advertising initiatives for two national membership organizations. Following that, I've spent nearly two decades as a consultant to Fortune 500 companies, start-ups, government agencies and nonprofits. In each of these situations, I've seen both executives and front-line personnel struggle to get their points across and the trouble that ensues when they don't. I've seen the power of great messages, delivered well, to open new business opportunities, bring about positive change and touch people's lives.

I've also heard and lived great stories along the way. Some of them are included here. But I also strongly believe there are rules for telling stories. In many cases in this book, I have changed names to protect privacy and confidentiality. In other cases, I was given permission to share accounts, and I'm grateful to those people who shared their stories to enrich others.

I wrote this book for you, smart people—executives, leaders and emerging leaders—who are frustrated that others don't see, don't understand and don't believe in all that you are and all that you do. For you to be understood, you have to communicate well. You have to remove the fog and reveal your gifts so that bosses, clients and investors flock to you like the 30,000 climbers who ascend Mont Blanc every year.

In *Prism of Value*, I'll introduce you to a way to frame and organize your communication based on a simple equation. I hope that after you read *Prism of Value*, you'll have a roadmap to guide you toward more effective outreach and connection that leads to the work you want, more satisfying relationships on the job and at home, and the power to realize your full potential.

Part I

Your Success through a Prism of Value

Chapter 1

What's Important *To* You Is What's Important *About* You

It was an ordinary day that began with a business networking breakfast. Standing in the buffet line, I struck up a conversation with the woman ahead of me about the eggs. She thought the scrambled eggs were real. I had my doubts, convinced that the gelatinous yellow heap on the steam table was the powdered variety. As the conversation drifted to the inevitable, "What sort of work do you do?" my phone rang. It was my brother, Lewis. It was unusual for him to call during the day, so I decided to take the call and stepped away to find a quiet corner.

He said just two words. "Dave's dead." Tears welled up and I could barely breathe. Dave was my other brother, and his death was unexpected and, at 57, untimely. He had died peacefully in his sleep. It felt so unreal. I ran out of that meeting to the privacy of my car, carrying my shock and sadness.

And then began the arduous process of packing up a life: disposing of possessions, closing down accounts and getting used to the new normal without my brother.

A few months later, Lewis flew to Kansas City to settle Dave's affairs. He called me from the bank.

"You won't believe what was in Dave's safe deposit box," he said.

"What?"

"He saved *all* the cards and letters from friends and family. Do you remember the telegram you sent him when he graduated from business school? It was in there."

I was speechless. Most of us put stock certificates, jewelry, cash and car titles in a vault because these things have value. We protect them behind a two-ton door that's theft-proof, flood-proof and fire-proof. We have a special key that must be used in tandem with the bank staff to open the box. Safe deposit boxes have gravitas. They're meant for expensive things.

But my brother's box held no bag of diamonds, no wad of cash and no deed to a South Pacific island. No, what my brother had stashed away were warm words from the people who mattered to him. And he mattered to them.

My telegram of congratulations. The "atta-boys" from his bosses over the years, praising his hard work and contributions. The cards from his nieces and nephew, wishing him "Happy Birthday." Letters from high school and college friends, checking in and sharing news about their own lives.

As I started to think about it, they were *so* precious because each was an act of kindness, of good cheer, of celebration. As much as the Kardashians value diamonds and designer clothes, my brother valued kindness and helping other people. He valued relationships. For him, those bits of paper were like rare rubies, and as such, had to be protected in a bank vault.

In death, I saw Dave through a different lens. It wasn't a surprise, I just now saw more of him. Dave was the sweetest, kindest person I've known. He had a great sense of humor, even though he was a bit shy and preferred the company of books to people. He loved to learn.

When he came for the big family Thanksgiving gatherings, he took on the role of historian, recording on his big video camera. He asked

Life's experience tends to move us away from our fundamental value...

us each questions and filmed my children's antics. At the time I thought it was distracting. Now I'm so glad to have those recordings. His colleagues in the library where he worked for more than two decades adored him. Receiving the tributes after he died, and seeing how he had touched them, was heartwarming. Seeing how so many others touched him through the contents of his safe deposit box was just as moving.

As we grow older in our lives, society and work experience, all the times we have been accepted, all the times we have rejected, have taught us what we should believe is our value. Life's experience tends to move us away from our fundamental value—clouding not only what we value about ourselves, but also what we can bring to any table.

Dave's safe deposit box made me think about my personal and professional relationships. I started to ask two questions:

- What messages are we delivering every day that our friends, colleagues, clients and customers would find *so* valuable that they would put them in a safe deposit box?

- What assets and beliefs do we value in ourselves, our companies and organizations so much that we need to protect them fiercely, so we don't accidentally lose or destroy them?

Understanding your value gives you a scaffold that helps you reach your life and business ambitions. But mere understanding is not enough. We have to be able to get other people to appreciate and see our value so we can be successful, whether that is in finding a life partner, landing a job, building a business, or fighting for a cause. We can't go it alone. We need other people.

English playwright William Gilbert got it partially right when he wrote, "Love makes the world go round." In fact, relationships marked by a myriad of emotions are what keep our world spinning. Relationships drive our lives and our businesses. Seeing the world through a *Prism of Value* verses a *Prism of Me* is critical to engaging other people. That's what this book is all about. When you see yourself in terms of the value you offer to others, people will flock to you.

Relationships survive and thrive based on a perceived *exchange of value*. If others don't see value, there can be no exchange, and therefore no relationship. Value is defined by what you *add* and what you *take away*. That's why it's so important to see our relationships through a Prism of Value, always seeking to understand how we are adding something positive and reducing or eliminating something negative.

Effective communication is the key that unlocks our value to others. All too often, our communication is one-sided, based on what *we* want and need to say, not what matters to others. When we see ourselves and what we offer in relation to what our friends, family, colleagues and clients need and want, and speak to that, we connect and become part of others' lives, missions and purpose. We add meaning and value to others, and in the process, only increase and enhance our own value.

In his death, Dave gave me an incredible gift—the idea of seeing the world and the way we communicate in it through a *Prism of Value*. That's the gift I share with you.

Chapter 2

It's Not About the Drill

Harvard economics and business professor Ted Levitt said, "People don't want to buy a quarter-inch drill, they want a quarter-inch hole." And why do they want the hole? To hang beloved Grandma's picture on the wall. Or to put up a shelf that holds important books or keepsakes. Or to install a baby gate that will keep their child safe. While the speed and power of the drill are important, the reason people buy it is not for its motor or the LED light. Those things are important, but in the end, it is about what the drill makes possible. The drill is the means to the end.

I learned this lesson the hard way. My first job at *The Washington Post* was as a copy aide. Among my many uninspiring tasks were answering phones and sorting mail. This involved hauling 50-pound bags of pitch letters and press kits from PR firms that would end up in the trash. When I wasn't hoisting mailbags, I spent hours standing in front of a wooden cubby hole in the Style section sorting letters into the boxes for individual reporters and editors. It was hard and thankless work. As a copy aide, I was ignored, viewed as part of the furniture; nonetheless, it was valuable to me because it was a foothold in the newsroom.

A few months later, an editorial aide job opened in the Health section. I wanted out of the mailroom. I wanted status. I wanted to move my career forward. While this position would still be an administrative job, I'd be able to sit at a desk, wear nice clothes, work closely with a small group of reporters and editors, and get to write a few stories. I was convinced I was the person for the job because I had worked at Mass General Hospital for two years. I knew a lot about how hospitals worked, and no one else applying had that experience. During the interview, I touted my experience, my smarts and my work ethic. I did not get the job.

The woman who did later told me that she had focused in on the fact that the editor was returning from maternity leave. So in her interview, she asked about the *baby* and then emphasized her strong organizational skills that would keep the editor on track and able to get *home in time* to put her child to bed. The editor was enthralled. I was like the drill salesman pitching battery life, voltage and the easy carrying case, rather than the results that the drill would deliver. I didn't communicate value.

Communicating value isn't just a matter of finding the right words. It's about the connections you create. If you want to communicate effectively and influence others to action, you have to get out of your own head and understand someone else's most pressing, relevant and unmet needs.

Nike may sell running shoes, but its *real* value is that it inspires people to be the athlete they want to be. Starbucks may provide coffee, tea and snacks, but its compelling, differentiating match with the customer is the experiential value of creating a place for people to connect. People will pay more for a cup of Carmel Macchiato at Starbucks then they will at Dunkin' Donuts because they want more than coffee—they choose status and an experience of belonging.

Southwest Airlines may be in the transportation business, but its *value* lies in treating its customers with respect at every part of the journey. Surprisingly, Southwest is sometimes more expensive than other carriers, but the no-hassle, fair experience that Southwest offers is worth the difference. It also stands for freedom. "You are now free to move about the country," was its slogan for years. Today it personifies freedom by the way it allows its flight crew to be as goofy as they wish. For example, on landing, they often say, "We've enjoyed having you on board today, and we hope you've enjoyed being *had*." Which says to passengers, there's still a place in the world for their own individuality.

Failure to communicate and then follow through on an underlying promise can squander opportunity. Poor communication can destroy friendships and even marriages. In business, poor communication can cost companies billions. Incomplete, infrequent and confusing communication leads to mistakes, poor customer service and employee disengagement. Many organizations aren't even aware that they're communicating poorly, until they start to see losses in their customer base,

The irony is we understand each other less, and trust each other less, because we aren't communicating…

employee rolls or balance sheets. As brand messaging strategist Don Miller says, "When you confuse, you lose."

In today's hyper-connected, cloud-based, app-filled world, we have at our disposal more tools to communicate more quickly, more broadly, than ever before. We tweet, we post, we Instagram with hundreds of people each day. The irony is we understand each other *less*, and trust each other less, because we aren't communicating about what *matters* in a way that others understand.

That's because we are focused on the drill, not the hole.

Ask yourself:

- Among the products and services that you use and love, what needs or wants do they tap into?

- In what specific ways do they communicate that they meet those needs and wants?

Chapter 3

It's all About Relationships

Relationships are the foundation of all human activity. From the moment we're born, we form bonds with others—first our parents and relatives, then siblings if we have them, other children at school, teachers, coaches, bosses and so on. Our success in life hinges on our ability to forge and maintain bonds with the people we like and trust.

This may sound cynical, but when you come right down to it, our lives are a series of transactional relationships—short-term exchanges and long-term investments. At every decision point, all parties involved are asking themselves, "What's in it for me?" You're probably asking yourself this question even now, as you're reading this book.

We give something: our love, our smarts or our talent. And we get something in return: love, appreciation or a paycheck. Healthy relationships have a *balance* where everyone gets something out of the bond.

My parents were happily married for 53 years. Over those five decades, they raised four children, savored good times, worried during bad, fought, made up and took care of each other. My father, who was a brilliant physician, was the outside man doing work he loved and bringing home the bacon. My mother was inside, managing the family. My father made it possible for my mom to live the way she wanted, putting into practice her theories of child rearing, reading voraciously and volunteering in the schools. My mother made it possible for my dad to practice medicine the way he wanted and provide for his family.

My mother always used to say that sometimes the balance in the relationship was 90-10, 60-40 or 50-50, but neither of my parents kept track because they knew it would all even out. They appreciated each other for strengths as well as foibles. They derived strength from each other and together became better people. Together they could face whatever the world threw at them. When my father was dying, my mother asked him if there was anything he would do differently. His response was, "No," only that he would like to do it all over again.

Theirs was a story of meeting the physical and emotional wants and needs that are the binding agents for every relationship, personal or business.

We are friends with certain people because they support us when we're down, they're fun to be around, and we just feel good when we are with them. We buy brand-name shoes because they protect our feet with style that gives us status. We frequent specific restaurants because we get our bellies filled with delicious food and have a delightful experience in the process. We work for companies because they compensate us so that we can keep a roof over our head, develop professionally, and achieve dreams for ourselves and our families. We give, and we get, in big and small ways, every day.

In exchange for answering our needs and wants, we give companies, organizations and individuals our time, our money, our brain power, our passion and our hearts. We're happy to participate in these exchanges because we derive some benefit. But if it isn't clear what the return on relationship (ROR as opposed to ROI) is, we are less likely to participate. When we no longer get the love or support we need from a spouse, we get a divorce. When the mean boss continually belittles or mocks us, we find another job. If we must have the paycheck, we do as little as possible and frequently call in sick. When the brand-name shoes aren't cool any more, we switch to a different brand.

Our value is based on the perceived quality of the exchange and ROR. We will pay more for a BMW than we will for a Chevy. We will pay a huge sum for a facelift that isn't covered by insurance because it can turn back our clock. We will go the extra mile for the boss or the enterprise that makes us feel important and worthy.

Communication is the currency of relationships.

Communication is the currency of relationships. Our words, our gestures and our actions give expression to the powerful emotions that we feel but cannot see or touch. A smile, an outstretched hand or a kind word propels us to connection. Conversely, a scowl, an insult or apathy causes people to turn away. Effective communication helps others understand what we can give and what they will get as a result. It greases the wheels of our interactions. It illuminates our value.

Ask yourself:

- What return on relationships (RORs) do you provide your boss, colleagues, friends or family?

- What do you value most in relationships with the people who matter most to you?

- How might you want others to measure their return on relationship with you?

Chapter 4

Our Communication Patterns Begin at Home

Chances are, when your CEO criticizes the strategic plan you drafted, you're instantly transported back to fifth grade. That's when a teacher might have dismissed that project you struggled to complete. You knew in your heart it might not have been the finest, but the critical or disrespectful tone made you feel that you just weren't good enough as a person. You felt ashamed and angry. The teacher didn't explain why your work fell short. And if criticism was offered, you heard only disapproval.

Now, your CEO is criticizing your work. Her intentions are probably good (she's probably talking to you the way she's been spoken to by her bosses in the past). But you're feeling the criticism deeply, and your confidence is draining away. Talk about misaligned communication.

Our approach to conversation, conflict and decision making is influenced heavily by what we experienced as children. These patterns shape the way we see the world and our sense of what is acceptable and normal communication. It's within our families or our grade school interactions that we develop patterns of intrapersonal communication—the conversations we have with ourselves—and the way we communicate with others. It drives how we interpret the world and how the world interprets us. Like it or not, we carry these patterns into our workplaces. Understanding how those childhood experiences have molded the way we interact can help us figure out how to communicate more effectively in a variety of professional and personal situations.

Our communication patterns teach whether to share information freely or tightly control its flow. Whether asking questions is safe or keeping doubts to yourself is better. Whether we should be formal or more relaxed and show some vulnerability. And whether we should keep things private or share them publicly.

Communication researchers Ascan Koerner at the University of Wisconsin and Mary Anne Fitzpatrick at the University of South Carolina have spent years looking at family communication patterns and how they shape behavior and discourse. *In "Family Communication Patterns Theory: A Social Cognitive Approach,"* they write how they built on earlier research to identify four main familial approaches to communication, conflict and decision-making.

> **Our communication patterns teach whether to share information freely or tightly control its flow.**

They have found that in **consensual** families, communication is shaped by a continual tension to maintain a family hierarchy, while also encouraging free and open conversations. Parents in these families believe that they are the boss and must make the decisions. But they will also invest a great deal of time and energy listening to their children and then explaining why they've made certain decisions. People raised in these families tend to value conversation and develop problem-solving skills. Conflict is viewed as negative and threatening to the health of their relationships.

Pluralistic families encourage children to make their own decisions and foster an environment of free and open communication. Parents in these families do *not* feel they have to control or agree with what their children decide to do. Parents encourage children to speak their minds, rather than to conform and to be involved in family decision-making. People raised in these families are competent communicators and confident decision makers because they learn to be independent.

Protective families are characterized by authority and control that rests entirely with the parents. Communication is about obedience, so there is little explanation of decisions. Children are not encouraged to question. People raised in this type of family learn that conforming is valued. Parents don't encourage conversation and discussion. The children often lack the communications skills to deal with disagreement or open conflict when they grow up.

In **laissez-faire** families, there is little conversation and little interest in actively developing children's skills in decision-making. These families operate on the belief that everyone should make their own decisions, but there is little discussion or sharing. People raised in this environment rarely experience conflict; they are never in opposition with authority because there *is* no authority. By the same token, because there isn't much conversation, they avoid conflict. They often doubt themselves because they don't have the skills to manage the conflict.

Whatever family types we come from, we bring what we learned as a child into the workplace. Here are some of the ways they might show up at the office.

"Let me explain why you can't hire that person." (Consensual Family Pattern)

You have submitted a proposal to hire a new employee that your boss has rejected. He calls you into his office and tells you that he knows how important this is to you but he just can't approve the request. He spends 30 minutes explaining why—budget constraints, fairness to other departments, a general hiring freeze. All the while he injects things like "surely you can see the challenges here." In sharing all the reasons why you can't get what you want, he is hoping to avoid conflict by giving you as much information as possible.

"What do you think we should do?" (Pluralistic Family Pattern)

You've given your deputy the responsibility for creating and coordinating a huge pitch that could bring your firm millions of dollars. Your deputy knocks on your door frustrated and stuck. He has conflicting input from various departments on what the pitch should contain, and now he comes to you for guidance. Your response is "Well, what do you think we should do?" You talk with him about the options, then say, "You've got some good ideas here. Go with your good ideas."

"I'm not telling you." (Protective Family Pattern)

All information is shared on a need-to-know basis, and most of the time, management doesn't feel that the rank-and-file needs to know. You might have worked with CEOs or bosses who have critical information, but they only share parts of it. Or they don't share it at all, so they have more *control.*

"Stop asking me questions." (Protective Family Pattern)
Your boss gives you an assignment, but you have a different idea of how it should be done, or even if this is the right course of action. So, you approach the boss to discuss and he throws you out of the office, unwilling to even hear you out.

"Just go figure it out." (Laissez Faire Family Pattern)

You give your subordinate a project and he keeps coming to your office with questions and new ideas. You don't want to talk about this, you just want him to make a decision and get the project done. You politely say, "It's your decision, so just go do it."

Ask yourself:

- Which family approach best describes your upbringing?

- Which family communication patterns do you see in your family members, friends, colleagues, bosses and clients?

- In what family communication pattern are you most comfortable?

- What family communication patterns do you feel make for a more difficult environment for you? Why?

Chapter 5

Colliding with the World

My husband Bill is a civil engineer. He thinks precisely and uses words sparingly. When we first met, I would joke that he must be from Maine, because his quota seemed to be ten words a day. He also came from a family with a laissez-faire style of communication. He is independent and makes his own decisions. He also doesn't want to belabor a point with lots of conversation or dithering.

I, on the other hand, like to wrap my communication in a narrative with lots of details. I came from a consensual family where we discussed everything, where we were encouraged to share our feelings, where everything was on the table. My mother would explain and explain, almost to the point where we just didn't want to hear any more.

Coming from two different family communication patterns can lead to some misunderstandings and frustrations. When he asks, "Did you pay the phone bill?" my response might be, "Oh, my gosh! I had some trouble with online banking, and I had to call the bank and the person I spoke to was an idiot, and I was on the phone for two hours, but I did get it fixed and I got the bill paid."

Now irritated, Bill might say, "That was a yes-or-no question. I don't need to know about the bank."

I might feel a little hurt that he doesn't want to hear about my travails. In his mind, I wasn't giving him the information he wanted. If our house were a Japanese restaurant, he's *sashimi*—just the raw fish. I'm *sushi*— raw or cooked fish wrapped in rice. We regularly

… we must recognize differences and figure out how to bridge them.

have what we laughingly call *communications collisions*.

Each of us experiences these kinds of collisions with others who see the world differently and who have communications patterns at odds with our own. If we want to succeed, if we want to get our point across so that we are understood and get what we want, we must recognize the differences and figure out how to bridge them.

Knowing that Bill just wants the facts about the phone bill, I should have first answered, "Yes, the bill is paid," and then followed up with, "Boy, it was really difficult. Let me tell you what happened." Because I would have scratched Bill's information itch, he would then be more open to hearing my tale of woe. He'd get the information he wanted, and I'd get the emotional release of sharing my frustration with the bank.

From our families, and later interactions at school or university, on the basketball team, at our first job, with our neighbors, and from mass media, we develop *frames* that shape the way we see and react to the world. The people we encounter are similarly shaped by their families, their first job, their neighbors and the media. To cross the divides that these different frames create means we must learn to recognize and then adapt to different world views, especially when we don't have power or control over a given situation. Our ability to communicate is the bridge that helps us adapt.

Working at the American Institute of Architects in the early 1990s, I had written a lengthy summary of several meetings of its Design Committee. The head of the committee was in Washington for some of these meetings, and I took advantage of the opportunity to go over the draft with him. The first thing out of his mouth was, "I hate this."

Stunned and confused, I calmly asked what wasn't working for him.

"I hate the cover," he said.

Pushing down my desire to say something snarky, I calmly said, "There is no cover. It's a draft."

"Well, I didn't read it because I didn't like the cover."

And then it hit me. This man was a highly visual person. He thinks in pictures and sees the world in three dimensions. The plain black letters with the working title of the piece held no interest. It didn't fit the way he accessed information. Like Bill, he felt that there was too much detail. Had I put a *picture* on the cover, he would have been more open to reading it. I eventually did just that, and inserted more pictures throughout the document, so he could access the information. He loved it.

I hadn't changed what I was communicating, I changed the *way* I was communicating so that it would fit into the design committee chair's frame. He was the decision maker. He was rude and could have made more of an effort to understand what I was presenting. However, I needed his buy-in to finish the project. He held the power in this interaction and didn't have to change, so I had to shift *my* frame to fit into his. I didn't think of this interacting as diminishing my status or value. I looked at it as to how I was going to *win*. And in the end, I did. The committee used the report to advance its work for the coming years.

Ask yourself:

- How do you react to people whose communication approaches and styles are different from yours?

- Which communication approaches make you most comfortable and which make you most uncomfortable?

- Are there communication approaches that you find intolerable?

Chapter 6

We All Wear Framing Glasses

Imagine you are sitting in the marble lobby of a client's office building waiting for a meeting with Ms. Important. A woman in high heels carrying a stack of notebooks walks by and slips. The papers fly out of her hands and all over the lobby. Person 1 sitting next to you leaps up to help. Person 2 sitting across the aisle is disgusted because, after all, this mess was the woman's own fault. Person 3, the receptionist, just laughs. All three see the same thing but have completely different reactions. That's because they each came to the situation with a completely different perspective, or *frame*.

In the case of the hapless high-heeled woman, Person 1 leapt up to help because she values caring and empathy. Person 2 scorned Person 1 because control, self-discipline and sensible decision making are most valued in Person 2's perspective. The receptionist, Person 3, values being a free spirit and doesn't take life too seriously. To her, this situation just seems humorous. Each of these three observers sees the situation through three different sets of frames.

Frames help us make sense of our world, giving us meaning to what we see and experience. We build our frames based first on our own experiences over time with our families, friends and colleagues, and then from our communities and the mass media. We also construct our frames based on what we value both financially and emotionally. We combine all these influences to create a story that helps us understand what just happened. We bring frames to our life, minute by minute, incident by incident. We look through them, and then conclude: "Yup, this is what it is. This is how it is."

Complicating our personal frames are the societal frames that exist around us. Traditional and social media further shape our view of the world and the meaning we take from events. Especially when emotions are in play, our frames alter our perceptions and our communications.

Frames help us make sense of our world, giving us meaning to what we see and experience.

Trying to communicate without understanding the frames through which others see the world is like speaking Mandarin to someone who only understands English. You can throw the words out, you can raise your voice, but the other person still won't understand.

Let's say your teenager is trying to convince you to let her go skiing during Spring Break. She presents you with "facts": Dr. Good, the principal of the school whom you admire and respect, is an avid skier and will be chaperoning. Girls and boys will be in separate rooms in opposite sides of the hotel. The resort will provide ski lessons, so she will learn a new skill. The cost of the trip is only $500.

Objectively, these facts are reassuring. They certainly are reassuring to other parents and their frames. But you reject them. It doesn't *matter* that Dr. Good is chaperoning. It doesn't matter that the boys and girls will be physically separated—they can find other ways to get into mischief. Her facts don't address *your* frame, which is that skiing is dangerous and your daughter is accident-prone. You don't want her to get hurt. And $500 is not inexpensive, especially when you anticipate an eventual ER bill. No amount of fact or argument is going to persuade you otherwise, at least not right now. Your daughter would have been better advised to try to see this proposition through *your* eyes and speak to *your* frame. The person with the power controls the frame. Later on in this book, I will show you how to shift the frame.

Ask yourself:

- What experiences and beliefs shape the way you frame the world?

- Think of an issue or situation you faced at work or at home where you and another person disagreed.

    o How would you describe the frame or lens through which you view that situation?

    o What is the other person's frame, and what experiences, emotional triggers or beliefs might be influencing it?

    o How can you bridge your views with theirs to reach consensus or compromise?

Chapter 7

Value is in the Eye of the Beholder

When my daughter Natalie was 16, she coveted a pair of $100 designer jeans. All her friends had them and she felt left out. When I told her that the $20 Gap jeans she was wearing were just *fine*, she stormed out of the room. She and I saw the same jeans and placed a different value on them, largely based on the framing glasses we each wore.

My husband Bill came up with a brilliant idea. We told Natalie we would give her a debit card and load it with $75 a month. With that card, she could buy *anything* she wanted. The condition was that she was now responsible for buying her clothes, the gas she used in the car, movie tickets, and Chipotle after school. In about a week, she stopped talking about the $100 jeans because she realized they would blow her budget. She started prowling the thrift stores. We had changed her framing and given her a new perspective on value.

Natalie's desire for expensive denims spoke to something she valued on an emotional level. Those jeans meant more than fulfilling the need to cover her body; they made her feel safe and secure, and more importantly, feel accepted and loved by her peers. Wearing those jeans would confer status, belonging and power. They were a ticket to the "In Group." For the privilege of those emotional rewards, the jeans company could command a higher price. It wasn't about the pants, but rather, how the pants made teenage girls *feel*. Those who couldn't pony up were excluded from the club. At first, those needs created a value proposition that, in her mind, was *worth* the extra $80.

The value *shifted* when she was responsible for the financial part of the exchange, which changed her *frame*. True, belonging was important, but she came to believe that it came at too high a cost. In the end, she found gently used "brand name" jeans at a thrift store and shopped some lower priced stores for knock-offs. The side benefit here is that because of her frame shift, she wore the less expensive clothes with the bearing of a stronger sense of self and self-confidence. That posture signals to her crowd that *she* is the cool one because she has a whole other thing going for her—a defined set of values that *she* has selected. *She* is now the leader, not the person begging for the privilege of membership.

Now think about how this plays out in business. Why can certain lawyers charge $400 per hour and others only $150? Why do some nonprofits receive millions in donations while others scrounge for $50 at a time? Why will people scrimp and save for a face-lift or liposuction but complain when they have to pay the deductible for a routine checkup? Why is it impossible to get a table at certain restaurants when you can walk right into others at any time? The exchange involves more than just fulfilling our basic needs; it's how we are hardwired to make decisions, which is not always based on logic but on emotion.

Advertisers and marketers have known what behavioral economists proved more recently, our emotions—fears, aspirations and hopes—can hijack our brains and our buying decisions.

If you understand what motivates people, you can guide them to seeing your value. Effective communication paints an irresistible picture of opportunity and then opens the door to it, making it enticing to walk through it. Effective communication also tells the story of the negative consequences of choosing *not* to walk through the door. It's all about the *meaning* you attach to your message.

Let's say that you have a red box you want to sell. The people you want to sell to like *yellow* boxes and are accustomed to buying yellow boxes. If your message is, "I have a red box, and isn't it wonderful, and it's *cheaper* than the yellow one," you may get some penny pinchers, but you haven't given them a reason to buy. If, however, you say, "red is the color of courage, and people who face life full on, who bravely live every day, own *red* boxes. Did you know that yellow is often associated with cowards?"

Effective communication paints an irresistible picture of opportunity and then opens the door to it...

Now you've started to show that there is *more* to this box than just a different color. If I'm your prospect, and I aspire to be brave, then I want to associate myself with a product that taps into my construct of the world. So, I'm going to go for your *red* box.

Let's take another example: fabric softener. In 2015, Proctor & Gamble, one of the largest purveyors of liquid fabric softener, saw sales declining. According to a *Wall Street Journal* article, P&G has a 50 percent market share of the $1.3 billion U.S. market. Millennials, lacking awareness and understanding of the product, weren't buying. Additionally, better washing machine design and new formulas in laundry detergents protect fabrics from wear and tear without the need for more chemicals. P&G had to come up with a *new* meaning to attach to the value of fabric softener.

The company did some research and found that these next-generation consumers not only *don't understand why* they need fabric softener, but they also want to *limit consumption of chemicals* throughout their homes. So, P&G launched an advertising effort designed to educate consumers. Gone is the term "fabric softener," replaced with "fabric *conditioning*." The new term invokes another familiar product: *hair* conditioner. This demographic likes their hair to smell nice and to create bouncing locks. They understand what *conditioner* is, and its benefits. When P&G repositioned fabric softener, they hit several value points: fabric *conditioner* makes clothes last longer by preserving colors and prevents laundry machines from "crushing clothing with 60 times the G-force of a rocket launch and baking them in a dryer that can get hot enough to cook ribs." The promise: you'll save money and look good. The company was able to reframe their value equation. That framing shift has started to pay off, and sales have improved, with U.S. softener sales up 5% between October 2015 and the same time in 2016.

Same product, different message that spoke to value in the eye of their beholder.

Ask yourself:

- When sales pitches come your way, what do they think you value?

- How are they trying to engage you?

- What emotional triggers are they trying to activate?

    o Your need for significance?

    o Your desire for more money and success?

    o Your need for your friends to think something is cool, too?

    o Your fear of missing out on something good?

    o Your need to get others to agree with your perspectives?

Chapter 8

Stuck in the Prism of ME

Jane Executive stepped onto the stage at a mega-hotel in Washington. In her role as CEO of the American division of a Fortune 500 firm, she began by telling the 400 employees before her how well the company was doing. She explained that they had beaten earnings estimates, and she cited stats about stock prices and future growth. She thanked the mid-level men and women seated in the ballroom for their hard work.

Then she dropped the bombshell. Expenses were too high, so there would be no raises, and they would be cutting administrative staff. She was cancelling the holiday party. Even the Friday bagels had to go. She closed with, "Keep up the good work."

Jane left the ballroom feeling great, confident that she had rallied the team to improve earnings. But her staff left the hotel demoralized and wondering, "If the company is doing so well, why is the CEO cutting things?" The bagel wars began, as several senior managers refused to stop serving them on Fridays. After all, the bagels didn't cost that much, and the beloved Friday breakfasts brought people together. Jane's actions seemed to reinforce the ingrained feeling that she cared little for the people responsible for the company's success.

What went wrong? Jane was speaking through a *Prism of Me*. She framed her message from the perspective of what mattered to *her*—great stock and earnings performance, which meant a higher year-end bonus for her. This was not what mattered to her audience. While she thanked the team for their hard work, the employees felt that she had just stuck that one line in to check a box and didn't really mean it.

Most egregious of all, she failed to provide *context*, leaving out the critical piece of information—why expenses had to be cut. Economists and analysts were seeing dark clouds ahead. While the company had done well, they were concerned about an eminent downturn in their industry, so the cuts were designed to get ahead of bad news and prevent massive layoffs. Jane thought that by holding back the bad news, she was protecting people. The employees thought she didn't trust or respect them enough to be honest, when she could have rallied them to take on a challenge and figure out how to deal with it *together*. She made an arbitrary decision.

> **…the Prism of Me shows up in stilted communication that leaves our audience cold.**

Morale, already low, plummeted, and some of their best talent, the people they needed *most* to manage the turn-around, voted with their feet.

We all get stuck in the Prism of Me. We know what we know and we see what we want to see. And when we don't listen, or don't seek to understand what others are thinking, feeling or wanting, we miss out on connections and opportunity. We can also do harm when we don't mean to, bagel wars being the least among the losses.

In business-to-business relationships, the Prism of Me shows up in stilted communication that leaves our audience cold. We revert to *List-Speak*, mere rosters of services or products, and fail again by droning on about our capabilities, our people and our strategic approach—lots of chest-pounding copy about me, but nothing about you.

Unfortunately, so much of the customer service we experience is through the Prism of Me. The tech support guy at the cable company who's in love with his company's internet bandwidth vs. the angry customer who can't access the movie he wants to watch. These two are in a relationship connected by nonfunctioning cable service. What the tech guy sees and what the customer sees are two different things. One sees beauty and a cool challenge; the other sees disappointment, frustration and anger. One sees a wicked problem, the other desperately needs a solution. If the tech guy stays inside the Prism of Me, he will talk about switching, packets and other geeky terms. If he speaks *Value Speak*, he'll say the four little words the customer most wants to hear: "I can fix it."

When we are stuck in the Prism of Me, it's usually because we aren't listening to and observing others. When we don't get the response we want, we repeat what we just said, or say it louder, thinking that repetition will lead to understanding. To get out of the Prism of Me, take off your framing glasses and try to understand how the other party might grasp the situation. If you aren't sure, it's time to stop talking and start asking questions.

Ask yourself:

- Are the websites of your company and others that you do business with talking about how wonderful they are without talking about what that means to you, their audience?

- Look and listen for the I/We to You ratio. Count the number of "I's" vs. "You's" in marketing copy If there are more I's than You's, it's time to adjust.

- When you discuss why you are good for the job, or why a potential client should use your firm or buy your products, are you talking about everything that you offer and how good you are, or are you explaining why you will be good for them?

- Do you understand what your boss, your family, your colleagues or clients need, expect and want from interactions with you?

- What are the words your audiences use to frame what you do or offer? Do those words match your words?

Chapter 9

Prism of Value

My father always talked about Ronald Coleman—not the *Lost Horizon* actor, but a shoe salesman at the local department store. He was a kindly man who, if you passed on the street, you might not even notice. But, boy, did he understand how to communicate value.

My dad always went to Ronald, even though many other places sold the same shoes at lower prices, despite the fact my dad always sought a good bargain. He would pay more because Ronald knew how to listen. He knew my father's feet and understood my father's needs.

I remember seeing Ronald in action. He greeted my father with a cheerful, "Hello," chit-chatted about the football teams they both supported, and then asked my dad how he could help. My dad would describe what he was looking for and the trouble he had finding shoes that would accommodate the orthotics he wore for flat feet. Ronald would ponder a bit, then disappear to the back room lined with shoe boxes stacked to the ceiling. Then he would reappear carrying a stack of boxes so high you couldn't see his face. As he helped my father on with each pair, he would explain that shoes from manufacturer A ran a little narrow, so he suggested my dad try a larger size. Manufacturer B would probably be true to size, though they had recently made changes to their design. Manufacturer C probably wouldn't work, but let's try it anyway, just to see. He would describe the specific leather and materials used because he knew that for Dad, more information was better. By the end of the conversation, my dad would buy two or three pairs, because they fit well and because Ronald recommended them.

Ronald lived the notion of "walking in another's shoes" almost literally. By listening and focusing on his audience, and not on what he had to sell, he sold an awful lot of shoes, winning prizes from his company every year.

Communicating through the Prism of Value means a shift to what our target audience needs from us—away from what we *assume* is important to them because it's important to us.

A prism takes white light and refracts it to create Technicolor rays. In our communication, we too often lead with white light, that is, *all* the things we think they should know about us. When we offer our clients, customers or bosses lists of data or rosters of products

Communicating through the Prism of Value means a shift to what our target audience needs…

or services, we're blinding them with the glare of all that we think we are. We revert to List-Speak. Think of that as the white-light ray. That's your Prism of Me.

But if we *refract* our messages through a *Prism of Value*, and consider what our friends, colleagues and clients need and treasure from us, we connect authentically. Unlimited opportunities open up as colorful rays. Much more fun. Much more interesting. Much more compelling. We deliver memorable and meaningful messages. List-Speak through the Prism of Me causes us to miss opportunity or even to create conflict. List-Speak sets you up in scenarios of yes/no, accept/reject. The bold colors of Value-Speak invite co-creation, collaboration and creative brainstorming. The possibilities are endless in the many colors of the Prism of Value.

No matter how we feel about ourselves, our value in the world is activated by what others value in us and about us. Value is *always* a combination of two things: addition and subtraction. Our personal or business value lies in the positives we *add* (loyalty, skill, security) and the negatives we *take away* (uncertainty, fear, frustration).

Refracting your messages through a *Prism of Value* involves answering two fundamental questions every day:

- In what way do you *add* something positive for your friends, family, spouse, clients, customers and partners?

- In what way do you *subtract* something negative or relieve a burden that someone else carries?

Answering these questions, and framing your communication around those answers, makes it possible to craft messages that express *value*, and therefore connect with others because of what's important to *them*. The positive side of the value equation often speaks to aspiration, while the negative speaks to challenges, risk, or fear. Depending on who you're trying to engage and what matters to them, you will make your case more effectively by emphasizing the positive or the negative.

The *Prism of Me* vs. the *Prism of Value* plays out every day for every profession and in every interaction. For years, dermatologists worked hard to get young women to curtail the use of tanning beds, highlighting dangers of skin cancer and death. It didn't work. These young women couldn't imagine dying. They had their whole lives ahead of them. And even if they *did* think about it, they weren't *convinced* it would happen to them. A study by Northwestern University's Feinberg School of Medicine found that women were using tanning beds to look better. A nice bronzing, they believed, made them look healthy. When the doctors shifted their message to tell them that tanning could actually lead to premature wrinkling and leathery skin, they were able to break through damaging beliefs and change behavior. Now they were speaking of a threat to something these young women valued—their looks.

In the next few sections of this book, I will show you how to use the *Prism of Value* to clarify your messages, foster collaboration, commit to what matters, and finally to better manage and mitigate conflict. Being aware of the *Prism of Me* is the first step toward moving to a *Prism of Value*.

Ask yourself:

- How often do you try to make your point without considering the benefits or drawbacks to the other person?

- Considering a conversation or an interaction where you or the other person was stuck in the Prism of Me, were you or the other person spouting List-Speak?"

- Do the websites of your favorite products, or the consultants or businesses you hire, speak about your needs? Or do they tout their abilities first?

Chapter 10

Prism of Value 360™

Creating a personal brand that communicates and delivers value to others begins by looking inward at who you are and looking outward at what your audience values. The magic happens when you connect who *you* are with what matters to those you want to engage.

As we noted in the previous chapter, big companies as well as non-profit organizations collectively spend billions of dollars and countless hours on developing and maintaining their brands. You don't have to spend millions, but investing time and effort in understanding what you have to offer the world, and packaging it so others can appreciate it, can help you get closer to the people and the work that matters to you.

Creating a personal brand...begins by looking inward at who you are and looking outward at what your audience values.

That exploration begins with answering questions in two parts: first understanding what you can add and subtract of value to others and then what others want and need. The Prism of Value 360™ is an assessment to help define what positives you add and what negatives you take away or reduce, in a range of everyday business and personal relationships. Completing the POV 360 will help you deliver a clearer picture of your value to yourself and your family and friends, as well as to your colleagues, bosses and clients who matter most to your success. The second part of the POV 360 is a series of questions to determine what others value.

You

What are three words you would use to describe yourself when you are at your best?

1. _____

2. _____

3. _____

What are your passions? What things in life make you light up, give you joy, excite you and why?

1. _____

2. _____

3. _____

What accomplishments make you most proud? Think of a situation at home or at work that you were particularly proud of, where you made a difference, changed the game, or simply were just immensely satisfied.

1. _____

2. _____

3. _____

You and Your Family

What would your family and friends say they value most about you? What are three positives that you bring to their lives?

1. _____

2. _____

3. _____

What would your family and friends say about how you eliminate or reduce their burdens and anxieties? What are three negatives you subtract from their lives?

1. _____

2. _____

3. _____

You and Your Colleagues

What would your colleagues and work associates say they like about working with you? What positives do you add to the team and the organization? List at least three positives that you add:

1. _____

2. _____

3. _____

What are three stressors, obstacles or challenges that you help eliminate or alleviate? What negatives that stand in the way of your colleagues' success do you eliminate or remove? List at least three negatives that you subtract:

1. _____
   _____

2. _____
   _____

3. _____
   _____

You and Your Bosses

What would your boss say you contribute positively to your department and the organization? What might your boss say he/she likes most about working with you? List at least three positives you add:

1. _____

2. _____

3. _____

What are three stressors, obstacles or challenges that your boss would say you help eliminate or alleviate? What negatives that stand in the way of your boss do you remove? List at least three negatives you subtract.

1. _____

2. _____

3. _____

You and Your Clients/Customers/Investors/Partners/Supporters
(Ask yourself these questions first. Then ask Clients/Customers/
Investors/Partners/Supporters the same questions. See if the same
ideas come forward.)

My customers/clients/partners/investors like working with me because of
the positives I contribute to their success. List at least three positives you
add:

1. _____

2. _____

3. _____

My customers/clients/partners/investors like working with me because I eliminate negatives that complicate or impede their success.
List at least three negatives you subtract:

1. _____

2. _____

3. _____

Your Value

Thinking about your most successful work engagements, what are
three words that colleagues or clients might use to describe the value
you brought them?

1. _____

2. _____

3. _____

Thinking about your most successful work experiences, what are three words you would use that describe your ideal work situation and environment.

1. _____

2. _____

3. _____

Your Impression

The great poet Maya Angelou once said, "People won't remember what you said or did but how you made them feel."

- How do you think you make others around you feel?

- How would your friends and family describe how you make them feel?

- How would your colleagues describe how you make them feel?

- How would your boss describe how you make him/her feel?

- How would clients/investors/partners describe how you make them feel?

- How do *you* want to make others feel when they are around you?

After looking at the answers to these questions, you will likely see a number of words that repeat. List the ones that show up across all groups. These are the ideas that you will want to build on when you describe yourself or your organization.

If your impressions are different from those of others, you will have clear sense that what you want to project isn't what others are seeing. You will have a sense of the gap and can determine how to close it.

Looking Outward

As you think about connecting with and engaging others, focus on honing in on their emotional needs and desires. You can do this by asking questions and listening carefully to their answers. If you are visiting a potential client at their office, look at what's on their desk. Is it a picture of their family? Are they at a beautiful lake? Then ask them about where that picture was taken and about that trip. That simple question can unlock valuable insight and information about the other person. You can also learn a lot by watching how they interact with their bosses and subordinates. Here are a few questions for you to consider. Don't ask these questions as framed below, but use them as a guide for how to assess others.

- What three things give your partners, clients and bosses joy?

- What are three of their major stressors?

- What are the things that drive them forward?

- What patterns of behavior do they exhibit? Are they always on time or running late? Are their responses short and to the point, or do they pepper their conversations with stories?

- From your observations, what matters most to them? Productivity? Looking good in front of their bosses? Not crossing the line? Pushing the boundaries of conformity? Being creative?

- How do they make you feel? Confident or on the defensive? Appreciated or ignored?

Chapter 11

Fear, Uncertainty and Doubt Cloud Our Value

Early in my career, I had to give a presentation to a group of more than 100 chapter leaders at the American Institute of Architects. I always prided myself on my strong public speaking skills, so I stepped up onto the podium with lots of false confidence and no notes. I looked out at the crowd of faces and knew I was in trouble. My heart was racing, my hands started to shake. I was overcome by fear. My mind was racing, as doubtful self-talk flooded in. "I'm really not good enough. These people are so much more talented than I am. How could I possibly belong here?"

I took a deep breath and began my presentation, which started off reasonably well. Halfway through, my mind went blank. Because I had no notes or PowerPoint, there was nothing to jog my memory. It was obvious that I was blowing it. The audience started to get restless and somehow I managed to bumble my way through. I sat down in shame next to the VP of Government Affairs. She smiled, and I thought she was going to offer words of comfort. Instead, she suggested I take a public speaking course.

Fear is one of our most powerful emotions. Fear protects us. Fear channeled properly can motivate us to move forward. But when we allow it to take over, fear shuts us down. As George Washington University Communications Professor Jean Miller likes to say, "Butterflies are okay as long we get them to fly in formation." When our fear runs wild, we lose control.

When stressed, our bodies become flooded with powerful hormones, including adrenaline and cortisol, which speed up our heart and increase blood flow. In the early days of human evolution, when our biggest threats were largely physical—a tiger or bear that might tear us limb-from-limb—these chemicals coursing through our bodies gave us the extra strength and energy to either fight our enemy or run from it.

In our business and personal lives, we face threats of a more psychological nature, like the high-pressure job interview or a high-stakes conflict with a spouse or friend. When we feel threatened or scared because our boss is dis-

If we don't know how to tame fear, it paralyzes us.

tressed that we missed a deadline, or when a friend is angry, hormones kick in, and our fear, uncertainty and doubt grow.

If we don't know how to tame fear, it paralyzes us. Worse yet, others can use fear to manipulate. In fact, the phrase *fear, uncertainty and doubt*, or the FUD Factor, is a sales and marketing reference used heavily by software and computer companies, as well as other companies, to scare people into buying a product.

Allstate Insurance used the FUD Factor when it created the "Mayhem" character. In one commercial, the character, his face wrapped in bandages, is driving his car away from a sports stadium. He says he's a referee who made a controversial call during a football game and upset fans chase him. He drives wildly through a residential neighborhood taking out an innocent homeowner's white picket fence, flowerbeds and lawn. Then the actor tells you that if you have another company's cut-rate insurance, you'll end up paying for this "mayhem."

The message goes right to your lizard brain—the part designed to keep you safe. This part of our brain will override our more rational side every time because we are wired for self-preservation.

On a personal level, our own internal sales person preys on our deepest fears and doubts. Interviews with high-achieving people, such as actress Meryl Streep, marketing guru Seth Godin, or Facebook executive Sheryl Sandberg, all reveal that each has doubts about their success. But they don't let fears or doubts hold them back. They learn to listen to them, then push them down and move forward. They channel their fears to keep fighting rather than to run away from opportunity and possibility.

Exhibiting fear can undermine your value in the eyes of others because they perceive it as a lack of confidence. If during a consultation with a surgeon, his palms are sweaty and he seems nervous about your upcoming kidney transplant, would you want him operating on you? Probably not. If you are in a job interview and you are shaking and your voice is thin, you will be projecting anxiety and likely will turn off the hiring manager.

The best way to squash fear is to take action. The best way to do that is to remember the *good* you can bring to the situation and how you might alleviate what is *bad*. When you look at any high-stakes situation through the *Prism of Value*, you build confidence to shield you from any psychological spears thrown inside your head.

The messages we repeatedly communicate *to* ourselves about ourselves can fuel our fears or can help us conquer them. Angel investor, author and inspirational speaker Tim Ferriss notes, "The best results in life are often held back by false constructs and untested assumptions." Applying the *Prism of Value* to ourselves to change the conversation in our own heads can help us wrestle our fears to the ground. It won't banish them, but by shifting our perspective, we can harness our energy to move forward to success.

Ask yourself:

- Thinking about situations where you have been stressed, what are the conversations going on in your head? What are those fears? What do you think will happen?

- Looking at your list, how could you reframe those fears in a more positive way? If, for example, you are afraid of embarrassing yourself when making a presentation, imagine yourself nailing it. Or if you are afraid that your boss will be disappointed because the project is late, think about how you can acknowledge the problem and what you can do to solve it?

Part II

Clarity: Your Communications Superpower

Chapter 12

Finding Clarity (or Focusing Your Communications Lens)

In the movie *Deconstructing Harry*, one of the characters, Mel, played by Robin Williams, is an actor about to shoot a scene. The cameraman is agitated because Mel looks blurry. The cameraman thinks at first that there must be something wrong with his lenses. Soon, however, he realizes there is no equipment failure. The problem is Mel himself. He has gone soft because he's out of focus. The director tells Mel to go home, get some rest and "sharpen up."

Many of us show up in our lives, at work and at home, out of focus, making it hard for family, friends, colleagues, bosses and clients to truly understand and value us. We are soft because we lack clarity. We haven't defined clearly for ourselves or the world who we are, what we value and what others should value about us.

When we strive to get along, be cooperative and be open to new ideas, we may not take on a strong and resolute posture. As a result, others perceive us, like Mel, as soft, a blank slate they can write all over. We need to write over our own slate with terms, rules of engagement, non-negotiables, values and expectations. Clarity helps us do that.

If your company or client is paying for your professional expertise and skills, and you appear uncertain, you will make people nervous, and rightfully so. They start to project onto you their own fears and insecurities. Or, conversely, they might saddle you with unrealistic expectations, and everything spirals out of control. Without clarity, we project a level of uncertainty, which in business can put you at a disadvantage, weakening your negotiating position and inviting others to steamroll you.

Furthermore, clarity is your differentiating superpower. If you are ill-defined, you look and sound like everyone else. Without a strong

Without clarity, we project a level of uncertainty, which in business can put you at a disadvantage...

stance, without putting your stake in the ground, you aren't giving people a reason to hire *you*, work with or for *you*, or invest in *you*. Everyone you interact with has limited resources and multiple options. Clarity gives you the definition you need to help them see that you are the best choice over anyone else, whether it's a date or a contract.

In the absence of defining characteristics, you may find yourself valued by others on price alone, your worth measured on how low you can go. Low prices work for big enterprises like Walmart and

GEICO, but do you want to be the cheapest alternative? The cheap date? The commoditized talent?

Clarity also helps you make the best choices for yourself. If you're happy to land just any job, you may end up working with or for an enterprise that isn't satisfying to you. Or you find yourself in the company of people who don't treat you well. Clarity helps you define the ideal relationship. Consultants just starting out or working to refresh their practice are often coached to define their "ideal client." You can and should use clarity to define your ideal workplace, company mission, culture or relationship. Then you'll know with great specificity what to look for and what to dismiss, instead of taking any job or relationship that comes along.

Clarity is the cornerstone of effective communication. Sharpening up involves work: introspection, reflection, focus and decision-making. Defining your clarity means making choices, closing some doors while opening others. You are going through an exercise in self-defining that companies all over the world do. Only in their world, it's called *branding*. Since they spend millions of dollars annually in this journey, clearly, it's valuable to them. So, why not take a page from their book?

Good branding isn't about creating a cool logo or tagline. It involves finding that singular hook that defines and differentiates a company (or you). Branding is about finding and expressing clarity. We can learn a lot from companies who have established strong brands. They're clear about what they *do*, and more importantly, what they *don't* do. You go to McDonald's to get a quick meal that fills you up without breaking the bank. You don't go there for fine dining. You go to LensCrafters to buy glasses. You wouldn't go there to buy a suit and shoes for a job interview. By clearly defining what they do, these companies don't waste time and money courting people who don't want what they have to offer.

Clarity gives you power. When you have done the work to define yourself, you can own the conversation, the vocabulary and terms of discussion. Chances are, the people you are dealing with haven't done the work to sharpen up, so *they* are out of focus. *They* are the blank slate. With this power, you can be the one to set the terms. Just be a force for good.

There is a lot of talk today about creating a personal brand. Go to Amazon or your local bookstore and you will find dozens of books written by experts showing you how to create your brand. These books place a heavy emphasis on creating a memorable personal tagline, having a good elevator pitch, or developing a signature look. But when you get right down to it, a personal brand is about having a clear and unshakeable sense about how you want to relate to the world and how the world should relate to you. It's about defining what makes you, well, you. What you will go to the mat for and what you won't. And how you will lead your life.

The *Prism of Value* offers a framework to help you find that clarity, not just by looking inward, but also by looking at how you project yourself. You want to send out the right messages to attract the ideal relationships and the kinds of work environments where you want to be. By doing so, you can thrive and contribute to people who will get what you have to offer and appreciate it.

Chapter 13
The Line You Will Not Cross

On a steamy August day in 1987, a helicopter carrying a photogra-
pher, his friend and a representative from a realty company that
commissioned the aerial photo shoot crashed into the Potomac River,
killing all three passengers. As a young reporter-intern at *The
Washington Post*, I was sent to the George Washington University
Hospital to get quotes from grieving families. I camped out with all
the local television crime reporters waiting for families to come out so
I might have a quick word. I was there most of the day, when finally
the hospital PR representative told us the families had gone home,
exiting through the back door. The pilot, who had survived, was in
critical condition with a broken back and in for a long hospital stay.
His wife was with him.

Relieved, I called my editor and gave him the update, thinking I was
done. He told me to try to find the pilot's wife and see if I could get a

quote. That was my moment of great clarity. I had stepped up to a line I wouldn't cross. I knew I *could* have done it. I worked in a hospital before I moved to Washington and I understood how they functioned. But I didn't want to. What was I going to ask the pilot's wife? Why did he bail out when three others died? How did she feel? As young and ambitious as I was, I knew that barging into her life right then would have been monstrous.

I walked around the block a few times, went back to the *Post* and told my editor that a hospital guard recognized me and wouldn't let me in. Yes, it was a lie, but one I needed to tell to preserve my standing in the newsroom. I knew I could do this once but never again. I also knew right then—with extraordinary clarity—that I didn't want to pursue a career in journalism. I wasn't going to like who I would have to become to be a reporter. My values of truth and respect for privacy seemed to collide with what I was being asked to do. I had trouble parachuting into people's lives, sometimes at their worst moment, getting what I needed, and then moving on. I had trouble talking with people who were not

> **Finding clarity is about understanding the values upon which you want to live.**

politicians or celebrities, who unwillingly found themselves thrust into the spotlight, not fully appreciating what "going public" might ultimately mean to them. I had trouble exploiting others' pain as "truth seeking."

Don't get me wrong. I value and am deeply grateful for the courageous journalists who uncover misdeeds and bring us important news and information. I just wasn't cut out to be one myself. That was the day I discovered there would be no more lying to myself about my future. That was the day of clarity.

Finding clarity is about understanding the values upon which you want to live. It is as much about what you won't do as it is about what you will do. Understanding your values and truly living by them, no matter what, makes you authentic.

Authenticity is the new cool. In a world filled with lies, half-truths and dishonesty, companies and individuals who appear to speak the truth, warts and all, earn our respect, gratitude and trust. These days, honesty is refreshing because it seems so rare.

United Therapeutics, a groundbreaking biotechnology company led by Martine Rothblatt, runs on honesty. When she built her headquarters near Washington 20 years ago, she asked the architects and contractors to etch the corporate values and objectives on a granite wall in the lobby. People around her discouraged her from doing so because it would be impossible to erase. But that was the point. In fact, the engraver guaranteed that it would last for two million years. The company values of honesty and respect for patients are core to United Therapeutics. Rothblatt believes that if you are changing what you say from day to day and change your values based on the situation, then it's hard to build trust among the team or, for that matter, anyone else.

Being authentic doesn't mean giving up your privacy and being fully transparent all the time. For example, you wouldn't go into a job interview and express your doubts as to whether you can handle the bigger role. Of course, you have doubts. But if you express them so sharply, you won't even get the chance to see what you can do. Imagine, if during World War II, Winston Churchill or Franklin Roosevelt had told the Brits and Americans they weren't sure they could win the war. Would anyone have followed?

Having clarity around your values, the lines you will and will not cross, will guide your actions and your words. It will also save you a lot of time because people will know not to come to you with certain requests at the outset. Knowing those lines is what makes you authentic and enhances your value to those who matter most.

Ask yourself:

- Where do you draw the lines about what you will and will not accept?

- What do you hold so sacred that you won't compromise, in any situation, even if it means not winning the job or the client?

- In what situations would you bend your lines and why?

Chapter 14

It Starts with the Message

Tony Robbins, the performance coach, author and philanthropist, has built a $6 billion empire on a powerful message: "You can be the person you want to be when you understand what drives you and others." Backed by neuroscience and propelled into popular consciousness by Robbins' larger-than-life personality, he has deeply touched millions of people world-wide who have found strength and the power and means to change their lives for the better.

Only Tony Robbins can be Tony Robbins, but we can draw life-changing inspiration from his message. Each day we can expand our reach to achieve our goals. Having the right message helps the world see *who* we are, *what* we stand for and *why* they want to engage with us. Sadly, too many of us don't invest the time and effort to figure out our message. We focus so much on the skills we bring to the marketplace, we forget to help our prospects understand *how* our skills can *serve* them.

In business, I've seen many companies spend thousands of dollars on a website, brochures, and marketing videos that fall flat. You could have William Shakespeare write your copy and Leonardo Da Vinci illustrate it, but if the message doesn't connect with your customers' needs, people will click away or delete your beautiful newsletter and find something that does.

It's not what you do, it's how you *serve* that brings value to your relationships. If you go to a networking event and meet someone new, chances are at some point they'll ask, "What do you do?" Your answer might be, "I'm a teacher" (or an accountant, or whatever your profession is). Their response might be, "Oh, that's nice," and then the person moves on to someone they think is more interesting. You've talked about your job title, but not about what impact you have on people. What if, instead of naming your profession, you said, "I open up the world to sixth graders," or "I show people how to keep more of their hard-earned money." These messages invite people into your world and ignite their curiosity as to how you might benefit them.

Finding the right messages about ourselves and our companies can be extremely challenging...

Finding the right messages about ourselves and our companies can be extremely challenging because the process forces us to slow down and try to understand how we actually benefit others. It's an investment, and it's a commitment and challenge that may require a shift in perspective.

If you've used the Prism of Value 360™, you now have a good idea of what positives you bring to people and what negatives you eliminate. Now the time has come to build on that and learn how to express it. Don Miller, in his excellent book, *Building a Story Brand*, offers a good structure for creating compelling and succinct messages that help people understand instantly how you can help them.

First, take a moment to thoroughly define who, exactly, you're trying to reach. Who are they? What specifically do they want? What do they need? What problem do you have the solution to? What do they fear? Be as specific as possible. When we ask clients who their audience is, they most often will say "the public." That's too broad. Think hard about who needs or wants what you have to offer. It doesn't mean that others won't be interested, but you have to hone in as much as possible on particular segments.

Second, think of yourself as their guide, the one who has the answers, the wisdom or the skills that can help them move forward to achieve what they are seeking, or avoid the thing they're dreading.

Third, think about what the rewards are for your audience.

You can express your value in three quick sentences. I call this the "They-I-They" model of messaging. Here's what it looks like:

> **They** have a problem: "You know how [most or many] [people, companies, etc,] struggle with, _____ and don't know how to _____?"

> **I** (or we if you are talking about your company) have a solution: "I have figured out how to _____. I have a process that _____."

> So that **they**: "Can be, do, have, experience, achieve, increase…."

Miller says that the most effective messages look at the problems at three levels:

External: Some measurable, describable thing they are trying to do—make the quarterly quota, hire the right people, increase sales, get the promotion;

Internal: Some concern or doubt about whether or how it is going to get done—"How is this going to make me look?" People will define the external problem, but what they're buying is the solution to the internal one.

Philosophical: The problem that "they" are facing is bigger than just that one situation or quarter. It is universal. The need to be appreciated, the struggle for acceptance, the challenge of balancing competing priorities. These are big issues for many.

The most compelling messages will address the problem at all three levels. Good messaging makes the people you are trying to engage the hero, and the problem the villain. The villain may not be a person. It could be the weather or natural disaster. It could be the red tape at a company, or the complex health insurance system, or the fact that they're not getting the raise that they've worked so hard to deserve. Whatever their felt need or pain is—that's the villain.

Let's look at some examples.

My friend Mindy is a health insurance broker. She could tell you that she sells health insurance to companies. Or she could develop a message based on the three levels that Don Miller describes.

The external problem Mindy solves is protecting employees with affordable health insurance.

The internal problem for the HR execs who are her clients is that they are messengers often bearing the bad news about steep rate hikes for reduced coverage. They don't want to look like bad guys and want to be viewed as a valuable member contributing to the business.

Finally, a good benefits package is part of the larger issue: recruiting and retaining the best employees.

What Mindy does is make the HR exec the hero by giving them solutions, information and credibility with the C-suite. Refracting her message through the *Prism of Value*, Mindy adds knowledge, comfort and solutions, and reduces uncertainty, confusion and cost. Using the "They-I-They" model, Mindy might say to someone:

"Many companies are struggling to keep pace with the changes in the health insurance market. It falls to corporate buyers to make hard choices that can be unpopular with both the C-suite and the employees. I help HR executives and senior leadership tame the health insurance beast. This way they can find the best options to keep costs in check, while providing decent coverage for their employees who then feel that the company is looking out for them."

Isn't that a lot more interesting than, "I'm an insurance broker?"

Let's take another example. Wainger Group worked with a Virginia organization that said it "Fights homelessness, one family at a time." We ran the organization through the Prism of Value 360™ and learned what donors, staff and the people who use their services all value most. It's the way the organization helps people to not just get out of the cold, but get out of the *situation* that got them there in the first place.

What this organization was *really* doing was building *self-reliance*. The **external** problem was homelessness. The **internal** problems were that these women had low self-esteem and didn't think they deserved something better. The **philosophical** side of the issue is that any one of us, under enough stress, could find ourselves adrift without a home.

The messaging we developed for this organization was:

> "Many people find themselves without a stable and safe place to live. But in fact, homelessness is the surface symptom of deeper problems. We provide women and families struggling with job loss, drug addiction or abuse that causes them to be homeless with more than safe shelter. We offer counseling, job training, a caring community, and other supports so they get out of the situation that caused them to lose their home, and become self-reliant and independent."

If you aren't sure how you add value, stop talking and start listening. Let's say you're at a business or social event, and you are meeting someone for the first time. Don't let the conversation degrade to the, "What do you do?" level. Ask questions about the other person and you will soon learn about their interests, family or work. Understanding what others are about will help you frame your messages in ways that will resonate, making your first "they" statement go straight to their self-interest.

To develop your messaging:

Review your Prism of Value 360™ to understand how you add value to people and enterprises. This will help you frame yourself not by what you do but what you offer to the world.

Think about what problems your boss, colleagues and others who you want to engage are facing and how you can help them.

Ask yourself:

- What is the **external** issue they might be facing?

- What doubt or fears might they have **internally** attached to this external issue?

- What about this issue **philosophically** is relevant to so many others?

As you frame your message remember this formula:

- Many people struggle with…

- I have figured out how to…

- So that they can….

Practice this formula and soon you'll be the most interesting person in the room.

Boring	More Interesting
I am a lawyer.	I keep people out of jail.
I am a banker.	I help people maximize their money.
I am in public relations.	I help people find their voice.
I am a real estate agent.	I work with people to find their dream home.
I am an administrative assistant.	I make sure our company runs smoothly.
I am a social worker.	I keep families together.

Chapter 15

Creating Messages That Break Through

Edgar is the Head of Facilities for a high-tech company on the East Coast. He prides himself on working with the executive team to create an environment where everyone can do their best work. One of the ways to achieve this is to understand how people use and move about their *space*.

Edgar wanted to try out some new furniture with sensors which would tell him when people were in a space, whether they were sitting or standing, and how often. He thought a good place to test it would be the R&D department.

Prior to the test, Edgar sent out fliers and left voicemails explaining the new chairs and what they would do. Jim, the head of R&D, was extremely concerned, almost paranoid, about competitors stealing his company's secrets. (This is a *good* thing.) He arrived in the conference room, reached under the chair to adjust it, and felt a bump. He flipped the chair over, spotted the sensor, and called security. He then ripped the sensors off all the chairs. He was sure they had been hacked.

Edgar later asked Jim if he'd read the email and flyers or heard the phone messages. Jim replied that *he never pays attention to anything from Facilities or IT*. Jim didn't value the messages, nor the messenger. Edgar had thought he'd communicated well. Edgar's messages were not framed through Jim's Prism of Value.

You receive hundreds of messages every day from advertisers, bosses, colleagues, family and friends. How many do you ignore? Do you have to filter out the low-value noise just to get through your day?

We must make choices about what and who gets our attention.

We must make choices about what and who gets our attention. We listen to those we know and trust and to messages that tell us something important, something we didn't know or that answers our burning questions. We ignore the messages that don't speak to what we care about.

People ignore your messages, too. Even though it may be their job to pay attention to what you have to say, it's your job to frame it in such a way that you capture and keep their attention. The person who fails in this dance is you. To create messages that break through, you must answer three questions:

- Why should your audience *care*?
- What about you is *valuable* to them?
- What should they *do*, now that they see themselves in your narrative?

If your message is falling flat, you're probably starting the conversation in the *wrong place*. You aren't alone. Most of us speak from the *bottom* and the *middle* of the communications pyramid where List-Speak lives, describing the *features* of our product line, or the programs we provide to low-income children, or the size and number of deals we've done. We are not emphasizing what we *add* to and *subtract* from the relationships we have with stakeholders. List-Speak without the context of Value-Speak falls on deaf ears.

To create messages that resonate, we must speak simply, and in short bursts. Journalists often talk about "sound bites"—clever, short, highly quotable nuggets of information that reporters and editors use to tease a story. We see it on TV all the time; short video clips of someone saying something so compelling that we drop what we're doing to pay attention to the full story, even if it means having to sit through a series of commercials before the news program returns with the promised segment.

Likewise, being able to develop messaging bites in our business lives is essential in getting people to hear and process what we want them to know and understand about us.

What goes into a great message bite? There are four elements:

- **B = Brevity:** Keep your sentences short, 10 words or less. Less is much better. Ask yourself: "If I had to pay $100 for every word I use, would I still use it?"

- **I = Impressive:** Your message bite must be memorable. Edgar might have said, "New chairs with sensors will help us give you the work space you want and need."

- **T = Topical:** Your messages must be framed in ways that are *relevant* to your audience. They must also have a sense of *urgency* so that we listen to them now.

  Edgar might have said, "Our company is growing and so must our space. Having chairs with sensors helps us understand how you use space now so we can create the right environment for you to do your best work."

  Here's another example. A Domino's Pizza commercial shows a man getting out of his car, just as tree falls on it. He frantically looks inside the car, sees the pizza intact, and happily extracts it from the car, only to slip on some ice, sending his pizza flying. But no worry, Domino's will replace any pizza you take out if something happens. You can see yourself in the commercial, maybe not with the car destroyed, but certainly dropping the pizza. The message is that we make sure you get your pizza, even if you slip up.

- **E = Emotive:** Your message bite should generate an emotional response in the person or persons who hear it. Emotion gives you an instant connection with your audience.

  Edgar might have said, "We know you're frustrated that you can never seem to get the conference room when you need it.

The chairs with the sensors will help us figure out how we might fix this problem."

Here are a few tips to create great message bites that draw on the underlying themes and ideas you are trying to convey.

Use Word Combinations that Clash

An MSNBC *Morning Joe* regular once described an interview with embattled Los Angeles Clippers owner Donald Sterling, where Sterling tried to dig out from racist remarks that were captured in a recording. He called it "apology porn." Those two words are rarely uttered in the same breath but, when combined, they create a powerful image that is memorable and speaks to a larger point about the inappropriate and discomforting nature of Sterling's answers. Another example comes from a client who spoke about how women are often sidelined for promotions because they step off the treadmill to take care of children or other family members. She referred to this as going to "Workplace Siberia."

Make an Analogy

Analogies compare things for the purpose of explanation. They're particularly useful when you are trying to convey complex information. They create an instant bridge between the familiar and unfamiliar. Comparing abstract concepts to the concrete makes your message as memorable as a rhinoceros with wings. Remember Forest Gump's famous analogy, "Life is like a box of chocolates?" Pointed, powerful and visual.

My med student daughter, Julia, once explained telomeres to me as "protective parts of cells that affect the way we age." Okay. But then she said, "They're like the plastic-coated ends of shoe laces." Got it!

Build in Imagery

A picture really is worth a thousand words. According to researchers at 3M, the company that created Post-It Notes, the human brain can process visuals 60,000 times faster than text. When we communicate, we often we speak in abstractions. We talk about things we can't see or imagine. We talk about departments, products, programs or strategies using neutral words. They might be critical concepts, but the realm of the abstract is slippery and easy to forget. When we use words like "tools," "tribes" or "guides," we create a snapshot in the audience's collective mind, and the images stick.

For example, an expert on dieting might explain weight loss difficulty levels by saying, "Many people struggle with weight loss because of metabolic issues that make it almost impossible to shed pounds." Or she could say, "For many people, losing weight is as challenging as climbing Everest. It's a long, cold journey that is best done with a supportive guide." The analogy, combined with words you can envision, creates a dramatic, memorable message.

Being able to craft message bites isn't just for the media any more— it's critical to entice and intrigue your boss and your clients with a message that sticks.

Use the tables below to start finding words that help you create messages that will resonate with those you want to reach.

Words that Communicate Value

Not all words are alike. Some words add value and others are just filler. Below are some words that pack emotional punch, both positive and negative. Use these often.

Value words start with verbs because they connote action. Action makes things happen. Verbs change things. Nouns lead the change, but it's the *action* where there's magic and emotion.

Verbs that Speak to Positives	Verbs that Subtract Negatives
Increase	Reduce
Grow	Remove
Expand	Eliminate
Create	Shield
Explore	Protect
Open	Close
Give	Save
Build	Break
Propel	Sink
Seize	Block
Succeed	Unblock

Nouns that Pack Emotional Punch

Nouns that Speak to the Positive	Nouns that Speak to the Negative
Opportunity	Challenge
Possibility	Frustration
Change	Change
Horizon	Boundary
Frontier	Parameter
Chance	Wall
Courage	Fear

Adjectives that Create Feeling

Positives	Negative
New	Old
Freed/Free	Stuck
Unfettered	Mired
Forward	Backward
Confident	Fearful
Strong	Weak
Powerful	Powerless
Encouraged	Frustrated
Successful	Failed

Verbal Pruning to Get Your Point Across

Keep your messages short and sweet. Imagine you had to pay $100 for every word you include in an email or conversation. It would change the way you write and speak. You'd be more succinct. So much of our discourse is filled with unnecessary words. Like an overgrown landscape, our sentences are choked with words that deliver little meaning, and not only keep us from getting to the point quickly, but also frequently *obscure* what the point was to begin with.

Avoid these filler words

- really
- very
- so
- sort of
- kind of

Chapter 16

Once Upon a Time: The Case for Storytelling

The four most powerful words in any language are, "Once upon a time…." We're hard-wired to listen and absorb information when it's presented through story. Stories have great power to teach, influence and connect us to each other and our common humanity. Marketers have understood the power of storytelling for ages. Think of some of the most effective commercials of all time: The Budweiser Clydesdale who makes friends with a cute puppy, or GEICO Insurance's dim-witted Neanderthal; even a caveman could easily understand the value.

Everyone…seems to have discovered storytelling, and so should you.

Everyone, from big business execs, to social change advocates, to management gurus, seems to have discovered storytelling, and so should you.

Use a story to help create your brand. The trick is to find the *right* story for the situation, and tell it the right way. Before we get into *how* to tell a good story, let's first look at the different *kinds* of stories, and why they work.

Annette Simmons, in her excellent book, *The Story Factor*, identified story types that work in business.

The Origin Story

This story answers two questions: "Who am I?' and "Why am I here?" The origin story establishes your credibility and engenders trust. Having a good origin story is essential for a job interview, if you're conducting training or presenting in front of a group.

While facilitating a retreat for group of government scientists and policy makers responsible for the U.S. nuclear arsenal. I realized that I had to establish credibility quickly. They were a tough group that included several ex-generals. They were skeptical about the retreat and weren't sure it was worth a day away from the office. I needed to build trust and establish credibility—fast.

I told a story about my father and the atom bomb. He was stationed in Japan toward the end of World War II. He had orders to be in the first wave of a two-part invasion of Japan, and he was convinced that he would be killed. Then President Truman dropped the bomb. I told the group of generals and diplomats, "I am here with you today because of the United States nuclear program, and what you do." Instantly, the group trusted me because I made a personal connection. Developing this rapport and trust at the beginning got their attention and paved the way for the group to get to work on the issues at hand.

Another version of the origin story explains your motivation and actions. Tom Cleever, a commercial real estate broker in Washington, wanted to raise as much money as possible to fight a disease he knows well because of his own experience. He was able to raise hundreds of thousands of dollars for The Leukemia Lymphoma Society's National Man of the Year challenge in a competitive effort. To do that, he told his own story for the first time since being diagnosed in college. He thought life as he knew it was over, but thanks to research that produced the drug Gleevec, he has thrived. He went on to win national college football championships and have a successful career at a global real estate firm. He wants to help others experience a full life. His story moved hundreds to contribute, including me.

The Vision Story

This crucial story answers the questions, "Where are we going?" and "Why are we going there?"

President Kennedy created a powerful narrative with his "man on the moon" address, in which he called upon Congress and all Americans to support the marshaling of resources to become leaders in space. That speech had all the ingredients of a great story. It had the villain (the Soviets) and the hero (us). It presented a Big Hairy Audacious Goal to land "a man on the moon and return him safely to the Earth within this decade." It laid out conflict because there was tremendous risk of financial failure and lost stature if we did not succeed. Finally, it offered the reward of being a leader and moving forward "with the full speed of freedom, in the exciting adventure of space." It was a powerful vision that advanced the space program, and in turn, the space program led to other technology breakthroughs.

Teaching Stories

Throughout our lives, we find ourselves in a position where we want *others* to learn a new skill or adapt to a new process. Stories are wonderful teaching aides because they help communicate not just what you want someone to learn, but also how to make it happen. When told through the Prism of Value, they also resonate most powerfully with the listeners or reader.

Some of the best teaching stories are Aesop's Fables, which provide valuable lessons in behavior. Think of *The Tortoise and the Hare*, or *The Boy Who Cried Wolf.* Real life also provides teaching story moments. A colleague once pulled me out of despair after I'd presented a report to a boss who savaged it. Peter took me aside and told me how the exact same thing had happened to him. He figured out the boss was a numbers and charts guy, and like me, he had delivered what the chief viewed as a pile of useless words. Peter took his report, put it in chart and graph form, and then presented it to the boss again. He loved it. Peter's story was a great lesson in presenting material in the way the receiver can best grasp.

Values-in-Action Stories

These stories help communicate the values you want your company or organization to uphold. All too often I read mission statements from companies touting their commitment "to the highest standards of integrity," (one would hope so) or to "putting the customer first" (you'd better!).

By themselves, value expressions can be empty words. With a story behind them, they come alive.

For example, what does it mean to put the customer first? At the consulting firm Booz Allen, they tell the story of the frozen suit. A consultant goes to Switzerland for a very important board meeting. He gets to his hotel and sees that his suit is all wrinkled, so he hangs it in the bathroom to steam it. He falls asleep, and when he wakes up, the suit is soaking wet. He hangs it on the balcony outside to dry and falls asleep again. When he wakes up, the suit is frozen solid, but his meeting is in less than an hour. He manages to force the suit on and then walks to his meeting just a few blocks away. During the meeting, the suit starts to thaw, making a huge puddle on the floor around him. The Swiss board members are staring. He takes a breath and tells them what happened. The men laughed. The chairman patted him on the back and invited our wet consultant to lunch. The Board saw how much trouble the consultant went through to put them first, even though he had set himself up for a humiliating experience. He was authentic, showed some vulnerability, and took a risk. His story built the foundation for a productive business relationship.

"I Know What You Are Thinking" Stories

These stories demonstrate that you understand what's going on in your audience's head and allow you to confront objections head on. I use these stories a great deal when facilitating groups that may be skeptical about the time they have to give up from work to participate in these events.

I like to tell one such story about a messaging session with a group of financial and real estate advisors who didn't want to be in the room and were itching to reach for their phones. One person in particular was groaning, moaning and disrupting. I made a deal with him to give the process three hours, and then, if he didn't feel it was worthwhile, he could leave. He kept his part of the deal and the session brought unresolved management issues into the open for the first time. My skeptic was so thrilled, he called the corporate headquarters and told them they needed to do this all around the country. I could say to similarly skeptical groups, "Trust the process." But telling this story illustrates why giving the process a *chance* can really work.

Storytelling is a powerful communications tool. Stories bring words to life, help people understand you and what you want to achieve, and engage audiences in what you do and what you believe. Stories bring others into your world and your life.

Ask yourself:

- When stories have touched you, what kind were they?

- Why did they make such an impression?

- When you're captivated by movies or TV or a good presentation, what is it about the stories they're telling that touches you? What kinds of stories resonate with you most?

Chapter 17

Is it a Good Story or a Bad One?

It's Monday morning at the weekly staff meeting. Bob, your boss, starts by asking how everyone's weekend was, and before anyone can respond, he starts to tell the team about his family's camping trip to Lake Getaway.

Bob describes in great detail how they packed for all situations because they didn't know what the weather would be. How he got out his father's old army tent and he showed his son, Billy, how to pitch it. How his wife Mary made eggs and bacon on a campfire. How they rented a boat to go fishing. How Billy caught a nice fish—a 22-pound trout. At this point, you are so bored that you wish Bob would hand you an assignment you don't want, just so you can get on with your day.

Now across town, Mary tells her team about her weekend. She starts by saying they hadn't been on vacation for two years. They decided to go camping at Lake Getaway because it was close, and there was lots to do. This was the first time the family had a little time off together. Bob is working twelve hours a day, Billy is on travel soccer team, and weekends for Mary are time to run errands and go to Billy's games. Getting out in nature without cell phones and other distractions was just the thing.

The weather was spectacular. But Billy and Bob were anything but. They argued the first day. Billy was in the midst of a FOMO (Fear of Missing Out) attack, furious that he might not catch the latest Snapchat update. Bob was having trouble unwinding. Both were rude and antagonistic. Mary was a bit frustrated as the domestic chores fell to her, although it was fun to cook bacon and eggs outside. They tasted better because of the wood smoke and fresh air.

The best part of the trip was the boat, she told her team. At first, Billy sulked. He was bored, the whole thing was stupid, and he hated touching the worms to bait the hook. As he complained, there came a tug on his line. Billy stood up, suddenly in a fight with the creature he couldn't see. For 20 minutes, he and Bob fought the fish together and almost lost, but with Bob's coaching, the fish popped out the water and onto the boat—a record-setting 22-pound trout. The grin on Billy's face was almost as big as the fish. Billy asked if they could do it again soon and thanked his parents for the experience. "Getting back to nature reenergized our family, and I encourage you all to try it," Mary says.

"Wow, can you give me the name of the lake again?" says Sherri Smith, the purchasing manager who almost never reacts to anything.

It was the same story—a family camping trip—but one version was dreadful and the other inspiring. Mary's story was about *change*.

Bob's was a list of activities. Mary's story touched a nerve with her team who also are living crowded lives. Bob's story was all about him.

The Three Essential Elements

What did Mary do that Bob didn't? She understood the three essential elements of a good story.

The Set Up

You have to introduce the characters and why you should care about them. In Mary's case, a harried family is getting out of Dodge to reconnect. Her team members have the same situation at home, so they can relate. While you are setting up the characters, provide a *time* and *place*.

The Challenge and Tension

In every good story, the characters hit a wall. They face a challenge. The obstacle can be a physical thing, like the moat that the prince must cross or the dragon to be slain. It can also be an emotional one, like unrequited love, the loss of someone or something dear, or a dream that's out of reach. In this story, it's the promise of peace and relaxation that isn't happening.

The Resolution of the Challenge and a New Equilibrium

Every story has a hero and every hero must meet and overcome the challenge. Meaning is achieved when a transformation also occurs. The prince slays the dragon and gets the princess and lives happily ever after. Billy catches the fish, and in the process of working together, father and son find pride and connection.

> **Through a Prism of Value, successful stories focus on "you," and not "me."**

In most corporate storytelling, the companies make themselves the hero, and that is where they miss the mark. The best business stories show how your client, your boss, your team is transformed or changed by their interaction with you or your brand. Through a Prism of Value, successful stories focus on "you," and not "me."

Ask yourself:

- In the stories you most like to tell, either at home or at work, who is the hero?

- How would you use the Prism of Value to tell the story?

- What is the challenge or the tension in the story?

- What is the resolution? It may not always be positive.

Chapter 18

Finding and Banking Your Stories

Walking down the street on a sunny fall day, I saw a gigantic tower crane sprouting from the middle of an office building that was undergoing massive renovation. Two American flags were flying from the top. I was transfixed because I couldn't figure out how they could possibly get the crane derrick into the building. Did they load it in by helicopter? How did they make it stable?

I mentioned this to my husband Bill, a civil engineer, who was baffled by my fascination. "They put it in the elevator shaft," he muttered, as off-handedly as if he was describing the assembly of a bologna sandwich. My friends in construction similarly couldn't understand my interest. For them, this was all in a day's work.

The wallpaper of our everyday lives may seem commonplace to us, but to others it may be extraordinary.

However, for me, on the outside looking in, it was something utterly new. Well, not *new*, exactly. But new to me only because I finally noticed construction cranes and started wondering what their story was.

The wallpaper of our everyday lives may seem commonplace to us, but to others it may be extraordinary. Our skills, knowledge and experiences become building blocks for the stories that enrich our lives, and that we can then use to influence others.

Unless we have the discipline to notice, we don't *see* the stories right in front us: the hotel housekeeper who makes a bird out of washcloth; the cab driver who overhears all manner of conversations; the doctor who eases the pain of an injured child; and temporary workers who know their city from a unique perspective because of the people they meet through short-term assignments. Everyone has experiences that can be captured and told to educate, inspire and connect with others.

Telling those stories *well* can help you build stronger relationships with family, friends, bosses and clients. When you tell your stories through the *Prism of Value*, you load them up with relevance and meaning for your audience, not just yourself. Those stories will make you memorable.

Let's say you are going to a job interview at an investment firm and you want to convey you are comfortable with risk, even when you are scared about doing something you've never done before. You could simply say that, but it will be much *more* powerful if you tell your interviewer the story about the time you bungee jumped on your last vacation. You might describe how terrified you were because of your fear of heights, but your friends gently talked you into doing it. You realized you didn't want to miss out on an experience that could expand your comfort zone. So, you climbed the ladder to the top of the tower, feeling like you were going to throw up. You didn't look down because it would rattle your nerves. When you got to the top, you were convinced you had made a huge mistake, but you knew that climbing back down would be worse. You took the plunge (literally), heart racing and adrenalin rushing through your system like never before. While you were bouncing up and down, you didn't throw up, you didn't die and you were strangely calm. When it was over, you were stirred, not shaken. Now you know you can do *anything* that scares you.

With a story like that, you show your interviewer you are comfortable taking risk and provide a reason to remember you.

Some people are natural-born story-tellers, but most of us are not. To get your storytelling game on, here are few tips.

Create a Story Bank

Just like a bank account where you put money in and take it out when you need it, a story bank is a collection of tales unique to you that you draw on. These come out of experiences at work, trips you've taken, advice you were given, and so on. You make deposits when you have experiences, conversations and situations that you would like to save, You make withdrawals when job interviews, marketing pitches or tense encounters occur where a story can really make a difference.

Making consistent deposits into a bank account can be habit-forming. In this case, you're building the habit of *story banking*. The good news is that you can make withdrawals, but your account never runs out. Your stories are always there.

Hunt for Stories

Think about times when you were proud of something, when you took a risk, when you stood up for yourself, when you went after something and got it, or when you lost something you wanted badly. Think about situations or people who changed your life or your perspective.

Get in the habit of asking yourself, "What if…?" or "How did they…?" Use your favorite note-taking system to jot down those questions and observations – even the seemingly insignificant ones.

Identify the Lessons and Truths that Your Stories Reveal

As you review your stories, put them through the *Prism of Value*. How does the story *add* meaning, clarification or understanding to someone else? In what ways does the story *eliminate* the confusion that might be in the way of someone understanding or believing you?

For example, the Tower Crane story is about stopping to notice what's right in front of you, not taking it for granted and appreciating the skill of others. The Bungee Jumping story is about taking a risk, stepping way outside your comfort zone and coming out well on the other side. The Frozen Suit story was about doing whatever it takes, but also about being vulnerable even if you look silly.

Categorize Your Stories

Once you've identified some stories, consider how they support your messaging and how that message is relevant to others. Then, categorize how you might use the story. Determine the type of story you're telling.

- Origin Story – Who am I?
- Vision Story – Where are we going?

- Teaching Story – Why and what we will learn?

- Values in Action – What do we believe?

- I Know What You're Thinking – Where are you coming from?

Categorizing will help you draw on your stories whenever the situation arises.

Learn to Tell the Story Well

Nothing is worse than a story that drones on for hours with too many facts. You want to provide enough detail and color so that your listener can jump into the story with you, but not so much that they lose interest. *The POV Story Navigator* worksheet is a good place to start. If you are in a job interview, you want to keep your story as short as possible. If you are in the break room, you have more time, but again you don't want to go on longer than three to five minutes. Look at the faces of your listeners. If you see they are losing interest, pick up the pace.

Raise or lower your voice, adjust the tempo or use your hands. Remember to paint *pictures* with your words. Instead of saying, "We have lots of strategies to facilitate collaboration among dysfunctional teams," talk about the "tools we have created that help repair broken teams." Strategies are abstract, but tools are not, conjuring up images of hammers, nails and wrenches. "Facilitate collaboration" is far more abstract than "repairing broken teams."

Practice

Once you've identified the key ingredients, practice, practice and practice. You don't want to sound overly rehearsed, but you also don't want to appear like you are pulling the story out of the air. Start by practicing in front of a mirror, or better still, a video camera or smartphone. Then, practice in front of a friend or colleague. See if

WHO IS/ARE THE HERO(ES)/ANTI-HERO(ES) OF THE STORY?	
Name the people who are the main characters.	
Are any of these characters barriers to the others?	
Time and Place: Where and when does this story take place? What is the weather like?	
Character details: What do they look like? Tall? Short? Skinny? Plump? What are they wearing? Do they have any distinguishing features or qualities? A tattoo? Freckles? Southern accent?	
What brings the characters together? Sitting next to each other on a plane? A fender bender? A family gathering? A work event?	
WHAT'S THE CHALLENGE?	
What does each character want? A phone number for a date? Your insurance info so you pay for damage? To be left alone on the plane seat?	
What is in the way for each character to get what they want? The other character? The weather? Boredom? Fear?	
What were the risks to each character by not overcoming what's in the way?	
What are the rewards for each character to overcome what's in the way?	they react in the ways that you expect.

WHERE'S THE ACTION?	
What specific actions does each character take? They simply say something? They move the other out of the way of speeding car? They just give a look?	
Describe a moment that stands out about the interaction. One of the characters almost gave up? Got frustrated? Hugged the other? Drove away?	
Describe how the characters felt about this experience and what stands out for them. Angry that the other drove away? Fear that they can't do what's required or afraid of the other person? Surprise that someone would be so nice?	

WHAT WAS THE RESULT?	
Did either character change? Their mind? Their situation? Did they decide to do something different?	
Is there a lesson or a moral to your story? Honesty does pay off? You can trust people? Don't talk to strangers?	
What might others learn or take away from the story to apply to their lives or work situations? Don't be afraid? Be open to new experiences? Help others even when it's hard?	

Chapter 19

You Gotta Be Shticky

In September 2010, singer-songwriter Lady Gaga showed up at the Video Music Awards in Los Angeles in a dress made of meat. Already grabbing headlines for winning in eight categories, including Video of the Year, Gaga's fleshy outfit drew even more attention and forever cemented her and that moment in the public mind.

People are attracted to that which is novel and unusual. Our attention will go to the red rose in a bouquet of white ones. We all like to think *we* are that red rose, unique among the white ones. "Remember, you're unique, just like everybody else." The reality is that few of us really are, at least not without working hard at differentiating ourselves in a memorable way. Finding

The race to the top of whatever field you're in is not won by skill, knowledge or talent alone. You need to find your "shtickiness."

something different about ourselves and figuring out how to communicate that can make a difference in getting what we want.

The race to the top of whatever field you're in is not won by skill, knowledge or talent alone. You also need to find something that makes you unforgettable and helps you stand out from the crowd. You need to find your "shtickiness."

"Shtick" is derived from the Yiddish word for "piece," but it came into popular parlance in the United States when it was used to describe the work of comics. Their shtick was their signature mannerisms or phrases. Today the word extends beyond comedy and theater to mean, as Merriam Webster's dictionary defines it, "one's special trait, interest, or activity."

Gaga's meat dress is an example. Or recall Rodney Dangerfield's hook-line, "I don't get no respect." Guy-Manuel de Homem-Christo and Thomas Bangalter, the two French musicians behind the group Daf Punk, were shy away from the camera. They found their shtickiness in a signature look and air of mystery by hiding their faces behind masks or helmets.

Shtickiness is not limited to the realm of movie stars and pop idols. You need a little bit of shtickiness, too.

We've been told about "sticky" messages—compelling enough to touch a chord deep inside but short and memorable enough to stick in our brains. When marketing ourselves, we also must have an equally clever way of presenting our work, our ideas, our products and our very selves. Shtickiness gets attention. Stickiness helps keep and grow that attention.

Southwest Airlines is very shticky because of its playful and fun approach to flying. At the beginning, flight attendants wore Hawaiian shirts, made fun of the safety check procedures and even played the sound of a horse huffing and puffing and its rider saying "Whoaaa," as the plane touched down and the pilot applied the brakes.

Richard Branson has applied his own fun-loving shtickiness to the airline scene with a full-on musical performance safety check video that encourages passengers to "buckle up to get down."

Do you think your line of work is too serious to have room for whimsy? Think again. Astrophysicist Neil Degrasse Tyson has it. Writer and author Gloria Steinem has it. Physician Mehmet Oz has it as well. Steve Jobs had it. So did Stephen Hawking. Each of these individuals achieved celebrity in a field far outside of show business.

Tyson, for instance, as one of the most eloquent teachers about the cosmos, defies the image of the nerdy scientist who can't relate. His clever turns of phrase have made him a celebrity among the real stars. He has been known to say, for example, that he didn't kill Pluto's planetary ambitions but simply "drove the getaway car."

Steinem, with her drop dead gorgeous looks, worked as a *Playboy* "bunny" and then wrote critically about it, setting her on the road to status as an icon of the feminist movement.

Steve Jobs didn't just like black turtlenecks. He devoted his entire closet to them as one more way to draw attention to a brilliant, break-all-the-rules business model.

Mehmet Oz stepped out of the operating room and the image of the cold, unfeeling surgeon, to help millions better understand their bodies. When you saw him pull on the blue gloves on Oprah, you knew you were about to see something fascinating (and, under any other circumstance, really gross).

Those who command "shticky" defy convention but do so with purpose: To connect and communicate. To be unforgettable.

You must find your shtickiness without being gimmicky, silly or over the top. If you are uncomfortable with what you do, you will simply look foolish. In business, especially in professional services, being shticky requires a careful balance pushing boundaries while not going too far. If a surgeon can do it without losing his stature, you can find your own brand of shtickiness without losing your credibility.

Howard Schultz built a sidewalk coffee kiosk into the Starbucks empire. Its persona reflects the business of community-building every bit as much as it does the creation of designer coffee.

Financial advisor and expert Suzie Orman built a wildly successful business out of nothing after losing $50,000 that her "big firm" broker invested poorly. She became a broker herself and found her "shtick" in something called "single premium whole life" that she describes as a "legal tax loophole that allowed people to invest with minimum risk and high returns." She gave seminars about it and wrote pamphlets and books about it and made a fortune. Her street cred? She started out as a waitress. When she speaks to her audience, she speaks from that place of ordinary-people commonality. Her shtick is that she's not above her audience, she just happens to know something that they don't; something that she's happy to share with them, friend to friend.

In the nonprofit world, there are many humanitarian aid organizations working in spheres that range from urban neighborhoods to war-torn countries. In the latter arena, Doctors Without Borders may be among the best known because of its fearless persona, going in first where others might not go to deliver needed medical care. Closer to home, the Salvation Army draws its greatest attention from the bellringers who elevate shtickiness to a noisy holiday tradition that's impossible to overlook.

So how do you find *your* inner shtickiness?

Coin a new word or catchphrase that can be associated only with you.

Economist Steven Levitt and journalist Stephen Dubner did this very successfully with the word "Freakonomics," a book title that laid the foundation for a new international brand. The book marries economics with popular culture to explore some provocative questions. They could have called it, "The economics of daily life" (yawn, yawn, yawn) but instead dreamed up a new and exciting word.

In my world of communications consulting, Heather Lutze coined the word "findability" to help clients understand the benefits of Internet search engine optimization. The shtickiness of "findability" led to a business and brand that in turn fostered a highly successful speaking career and book publishing enterprise.

Marie Forleo builds confidence in her audience by reminding them that "everything is figure-out-able." And we'd love to figure out who was first to pluck from the internet zone such shtickable words as "crowdsourcing" or "geobragging."

Capitalize on what's different.

I once went to a dentist who had majored in music as well as chemistry. He used his music talent as much as his dental skills. Once, after telling me I'd need gum surgery, he took out his guitar and played some Beatles music softly, which had the strange effect of calming me down. The singing periodontist. Now that's different. He is an excellent dentist, but he also has a different approach. I've referred him to dozens of people.

As another example, I once had a boss who always wore a red dress, especially when she went to meetings outside the office. Most of the other women were wearing neutral colors, and she definitely was noticed. Red became her signature. When she spoke, people tended to listen.

Promote. Promote. Promote.

Shticky people constantly promote their shtick. They write books, they speak, they take bold and provocative positions, and they consistently remind you of their shtick. They demand to be noticed.

Suzie Orman heard a "financial expert" on the radio give wrong advice. She wrote a long letter to the station manager, and a few weeks later, he asked her to be on his show. She then became a regular, promoting herself and her business.

Mohammed Ali was a great boxer, but he also had a way with words unusual for sports figures. His pithy, self-promotional quotes like, "Float like a butterfly, sting like a bee," made him the darling of journalists and set him apart from every other fighter. Mohammed Ali would constantly proclaim his greatness. Saying it often enough (along with his winning record) made it so.

Shtickiness isn't just about coming up with a signature word, idea, approach or promotion. It's an attitude and a way of being. It's about being willing to be different in a way that gets you noticed, makes you memorable and highlights the contributions you make to your colleagues, bosses, clients and friends. It's doing so in a way that is true to who you are and want to be.

It's also about delivering that line over and over again without getting tired of it yourself. Did Ali get tired of hearing himself proclaim that he was the greatest? Maybe. But he knew the power of the hook, and we're not talking about the boxing move.

Think about that thing you say or do. Or the way you think it's different. Or even that thing that is guaranteed to embarrass all your friends. And work it.

Ask yourself:

- When you think about people you admire most, what about them stands out? Do they have a unique look, turn of phrase or point of view?

- What about you is your signature? A colleague of mine loves birds, so in addition to wearing bird pins or scarves with birds on them, she asks during her trainings that people refrain from making bird analogies. Whether you like it or not, she is memorable.

- How can you turn a passion, a favorite color or a turn of phrase into your "shtickiness?"

Part III

Commit, Collaborate, and Resolve Conflict

Chapter 20

Communicate to Collaborate

"Working with other people just makes you smarter, that's proven," says Lin-Manuel Miranda in *Smithsonian Magazine*. "We elevate each other [and] it's enormously gratifying because you can build things so much bigger than yourself."

Miranda created *Hamilton*, one of the most exciting musicals to hit Broadway in years. The show is sold out most every night, and tickets can fetch thousands of dollars. He created something valuable and original, but he didn't do it on his own. He may have spent seven years conceiving and writing the play and the music, but to bring it to life, he had to recruit an extraordinary cast, set designers, investors and others. He was able to get his team to work well together because everything he did was in service to the show and to the people who were part of it. Not himself. The collected effort was in service to the play, not him, even though it was his personal vision.

When he was in college, Miranda had explored all aspects of theater, from sewing costumes to lighting. Because he understood the jobs and roles of his collaborators, he says, he was able to communicate with them more effectively. He knew he couldn't realize his vision all by himself. This team was critical.

Every day, whether in our companies, on a sports team, or with our families and friends, we need to work with and through other people to achieve what we want. Getting others to work with us in ways that advance our goals and visions can be incredibly difficult. Collaboration involves give-and-take and a willingness to subordinate some of ourselves to achieve something bigger, something perhaps even better than what we brought to the team originally.

The reason we're willing to do that is because we see an ultimate reward, an outcome that matters so much to us what we're willing to give something up in its service. The first responsibility is ours: To transfer the vision—and our passionate belief in the vision—from our heads into the minds and imaginations of the people we need to join in the effort.

> **If each of us is a brick supporting the foundations of our social systems…then effective communication is the mortar that holds it all together.**

And that requires—you guessed it—communication.

If each of us is a brick supporting the foundations of our social systems, our companies or our families, then effective communication is the mortar that holds it all together. Only with the power of our words and actions are we able to recruit others to join us and keep them motivated.

One of the best examples of team-building and collaboration is Dorothy in *The Wizard of Oz*. Dorothy finds herself transported from her native Kansas by a ferocious tornado, landing in the magical and scary land of Oz. From the moment she gets there, all she wants to do is go home.

For her quest, she successfully recruits a loyal and devoted team. Timid and frightened, Dorothy turns out to be one heck of a communicator. She convinces the Scarecrow, the Tin Man and the Cowardly Lion to join her because she has a great message: "I want to go home." It's clear, simple, memorable, and most important, touches a chord deep within them. They see *value* in accompanying her to Oz because they, *too*, are searching for their metaphorical home—a place where their desires and aspirations can be reached. For Scarecrow it's a brain, for Tin Man, a heart, and for the Lion, "the nerve."

Dorothy grabs them because she takes the time to listen and understand what they want, putting aside her own needs for a minute to understand each of their needs before pitching them to join her. Her pitch is made through the *Prism of Value*. I am off to see the Wizard and why don't you join me so he can help you get what you desire, too. It works. They link arms and skip along the Yellow Brick Road despite its dangers, facing trees who throw things and the Wicked Witch of the West and her flying monkeys who are determined to destroy Dorothy and her crew. They persist because Dorothy values them for who they are and makes them better.

She unwittingly had mastered the *Prism of Value* by listening to them, setting aside her desperate needs to hear theirs first. The Scarecrow, Tin Man and Lion each desperately sought something elusive: intelligence, love, courage. Dorothy links her heroic journey to Kansas to *their* journey, tying her message and her goals to something bigger than herself.

This journey has universal appeal because it's about understanding yourself and your place in the world. Finding that place is finding our metaphorical home.

Work environments and social systems can sometimes feel as weird, scary and exhilarating as Oz. Often what stands in the way of our success is our inability to collaborate. We fight each other, and then decide to go it alone because we don't see or understand that value of working together, and we don't fully appreciate what others can bring to our table. When we understand our shared goals and take the time to understand the internal and philosophical needs of our collaborators, we can work together in service to that common goal instead of sowing seeds of discord and frustration.

The next few chapters discuss how to filter your communication through the *Prism of Value* to foster productive collaboration.

Ask yourself:

- What situations have you been involved in or observed that are great examples of collaborative efforts?

- Why do you think they were successful?

- What were collaborations that haven't worked? Why do you think they didn't?

Chapter 21

Keep Your Ego in Check

Lance Armstrong was the darling of pro cycling. It was a remarkable story of triumph over adversity, inspiration, hard work and charity. After a diagnosis of cancer that had spread to his brain and stomach, he was given a 50/50 chance of survival. Not only did he survive, he trained and competed hard, becoming one of the best cyclists in history, winning seven grueling Tour de France races, the pinnacle of his sport. He set up a charity to help other cancer patients, raising millions and millions of dollars. He was flush with cash from lucrative endorsements from Nike and other companies.

As his fame and success grew, so did the rumors that he and other teammates were doping. Armstrong vehemently denied them, lying over and over again to anyone who challenged him. The rumors, of course, turned out to be true. All those medals were not won by talent alone. Like Icarus, who in Greek mythology built wings of feathers and wax, then flew too close to the sun, Armstrong let his ego get in the way, eventually leading to the destruction of his career and his reputation. Even when the World Doping Association investigators had proof of his transgressions, Armstrong, true to a pattern of arrogance, told them he'd cooperate, but that fair punishment should be a ban from cycling of no more than a year. Instead, he was banned from all sports for life, stripped of his titles, and cut off from his lucrative endorsements and the "good-guy" reputation he'd worked so hard to cultivate.

Unchecked ego can be our biggest enemy, clouding our judgment and communication. Our egos trap us in the Prism of Me and leave little room for others. Ego can't be allowed to run over ourselves or those around us, although it can help us get to where we want to go.

Look closely at highly successful people and you will find strong egos and an insatiable curiosity. A strong sense of self empowers people when all looks helpless. It's ego that sets a vision, no matter how impossible it may seem.

> **Our egos trap us in the Prism of Me and leave little room for others.**

It's your ego that whispers, "Go for it!" It's ego that pushes us forward, encouraging us to trust our intuition and move ahead, even when there are no indications that we'll succeed. However, an ability to understand that you are part of something bigger helps keep the ego in check, making it a force for positive things.

Ego expresses itself differently within different personalities. It's not always about being self-centered or tone deaf. Mother Theresa, Oprah, Steve Jobs and Albert Einstein are all associated with a strong ego. Yet each of them has been able to inspire others to be their best selves because they approach the world through the *Prism of Value*.

They look at themselves through a lens of what they can *bring* to the world. It is about them, but it's also about making a *difference*. They observe, they ask questions and understand they need others to achieve their vision. They also believe in themselves when they take risks, even if they fail.

By all accounts, Steve Jobs was difficult to work with, to put it mildly. However, his unrelenting quest for excellence and his push for innovation inspired loyalty. His drive and vision inspired others. Looking at it through the Prism of Value, an obnoxious personality might have been worth the price of being involved with creating products that truly changed the way we live.

Oprah's genuine interest in people and their struggles, and her desire to help, have endeared her to millions worldwide. Fans value her because she values herself, even her imperfections.

Albert Einstein was perhaps the most curious of people. His ego let him follow logic and intuition to scientific places yet uncharted.

While their egos drove them forward, they also had a deeper purpose—to serve others or a cause bigger than themselves. Arrogance can be forgiven if the source also serves a common good.

Regardless of the size of ego, none of these people, as smart and powerful as they are, could have accomplished what they did by themselves.

The answers to the following questions will help you understand your motivations and clarify the differences between what's good for you personally and good for the people and organizations with which you engage. If the answers tend to be more about you, think about how you can apply the *Prism of Value* to discover ways to see how your project benefits the people whose support you need for success. Then, speak to them through *that Prism of Value.*

Ask yourself:

- Have I looked at what I want and need in relation to the needs and wants of my family, friends or company?

- Have I spoken to them about my ambitions and taken the time to help them see how they will benefit from my focus?

- What is the common goal that I share with my family, friends or company?

- Am I doing this because it makes me feel or look good, or is it the right thing to do?

- How could other people help me achieve what I want to achieve? What's in it for them?

- What do other people need from me so that they can achieve what they want and help me?

- What's more important: Being right? Doing it my way? Winning and achieving?

- Am I seeking short-term, quick results, or am I thinking about building something—my family, my career, my department, my company or nonprofit—for the long term?

Chapter 22

Sharing the Fingerprints

Emily manages a large team at a marketing research firm. A major deadline looms and she knows there's only one way to find and analyze the type of market intelligence for the client. She brings the team together and highlights the urgency and the importance of the client to the firm. She also tells the team exactly how to attack the project.

The team pushes back, saying there are other options. Emily knows from experience that there are no other options, and she tells them to do it her way. Her tone and attitude signals there is no time even to have this conversation. The job needs to be done and done now.

Effective collaboration requires giving people the space and opportunity to put their fingerprints on their work.

But the team continues to want to explore possibilities. Frustrated and concerned that this big project is going to blow up, she has a flash of insight. This team needed to own the process as much as the responsibility for the outcome. She could either squander the time arguing or give them a defined set of time to come up with a better approach. She decides to back off her position and challenges the team to spend exactly one hour thinking through the other options, and then let her know what they are. The team worked together. An hour later, the team came back with the exact plan Emily wanted them to follow all along. What's the benefit of "wasting" that hour? The team now feels ownership of the project as much as Emily does.

Effective collaboration requires giving people the space and opportunity to put their fingerprints on their work. Leaders thwart effective collaboration by feeling, as Emily did, that they need to coerce teams to get them to function. Managers learn the hard way, or the easy, way that micromanaging is ultimately a time-waster. To her credit, Emily chose the easy way.

Alex "Sandy" Pentland, Director of MIT's Human Dynamics Laboratory, conducted extensive research that suggests the difference in high-performance teams is not the content of team discussions but the ways in which they communicate. By having team members in a variety of workplaces wear sensors to track both the frequency and quality of interactions, he identified three aspects of communication that affected performance: Energy, Engagement and Exploration.

Pentland defines **Energy** as the number and quality of exchanges within a team. When people are brainstorming or discussing new information, energy levels are higher. When the boss is updating on new policies, or even sharing the latest quarterly numbers, energy levels are lower. When Emily stepped out of the room and let the team work out the problem on their own, the energy was refocused from resisting to problem-solving. The energy was also heightened.

Engagement refers to how the energy is distributed among the members of the team. When Emily was barking her orders, there was little engagement because all the energy and momentum was with her. The key to successful collaboration is that everyone in the team talks and listens in equal measure, with no one person dominating. It also means that communication among team members is short and to the point.

Exploration involves communication with people outside their own team, whether that be others within an organization or external audiences, such as clients or independent experts. Pentland notes that the coexistence of engagement and exploration can be challenging because energy, like time, is a finite resource. Teams must find the right balance between the two.

In Pentland's research, the most effective means of facilitating communication was, not surprisingly, face-to-face, where all participants could feed off each others' energy. Second best was telephone and videoconferencing, though it becomes less effective with larger groups. Texting and email were the least effective.

The communication behavior that Pentland observed in high-performance teams and wrote about in the *Harvard Business Journal* included:

- Team members speak and listen in equal measure with no one person dominating the discussion.

- Members face one another, and their conversations and gestures are energetic.

- Members connect directly with one another, not just with the team leader.

- Members carry no back-channel or side conversations within the team.
- Members periodically break, go exploring outside the team, and bring information back.

Take a minute to examine how you and your teams communicate and interact.

If you are the leader, ask:

- Am I creating a space where everyone is encouraged to speak up as well as listen to others?
- How much of our communication is face-to-face versus email and text? Is it the right balance?
- When we meet, am I, or specific team members, dominating the discussion?
- Do team members trust each other? How might I encourage the team members to connect directly with each other?
- How might I encourage the team to reach out to others within our organization, as well as externally, to broaden and enrich understanding and explore perspectives?
- Am I relying too much on email and texts?
- How much time am I spending understanding the team and its members?
- How much of the process can I let go of, without losing control over the outcome?

If you are a participant on the team, ask:

- How well am I participating in this team?

- What am I contributing to the team?

- What does each team member have to offer the team, as well as to me?

- How might I go outside the team to find information and insights?

- Am I relying too much on email and texts? How else might I communicate?

- Am I listening to what others are saying and really hearing their points?

- Do I trust my team? What might be getting in the way of closer rapport?

- How do I feel when I do speak up? Am I heard and my opinions respected?

- What can I do to contribute to the energy, engagement and exploration of the team?

Chapter 23

Stepping into Someone Else's Shoes

I was attending a conference at a well-known Washington hotel. With just 20 minutes for lunch, I opted for the hotel restaurant, which was busier than usual. I ordered a Cobb salad—no meat, extra cheese—and explained I was pressed for time. A few minutes later, I saw a salad emerge from the kitchen and then retreat. Then the same thing happened again. Time was running out, so I asked the waiter what was going on. He said he told the kitchen, "No meat," but they didn't listen. Finally, the salad emerged without meat but also without cheese. After I asked for a manager to explain that there was a communications issue, her off-handed response was to comp my still unsatisfactory salad. It wasn't about the free lunch (if I wanted the money, I would have packed a lunch). She responded according to her value set, thinking that would make things right. She completely missed my point, which, as a communications expert and teacher, made it even more frustrating for me and expensive for the restaurant.

Let's say, conservatively, that this kind of misunderstanding—and comped meal—happens three times a day. Over the course of the year, that could cost the hotel roughly $17,472 in hard food costs, labor and lost productivity. What can't be calculated are the intangible costs of poor morale among servers and kitchen staff, not to mention the consequences of an unhappy customer who shares this story with others. This restaurant team clearly wasn't collaborating. Part of the problem was they just weren't communicating. Either the wait staff hadn't made the customer requests clear, or the kitchen staff wasn't listening. Maybe a little bit of both, or a lot of both.

To engage effectively with those who are most critical to your success, everyone on the team must understand their *purpose*. In the case of the restaurant staff, their overarching goal was to serve the customer, and that meant preparing the best quality meals (to order) and serving them fast with a smile. The food and service are the means to achieve the ultimate goal: a happy customer who keeps coming back.

Everyone on that hotel's team seemed stuck in the *Prism of ME*. The boss was focused on turning the tables quickly to accommodate the lunch rush; the waiter was focused on taking the orders and serving food; and the kitchen staff was focused on preparing the food. But they weren't working together to make sure that each had what they needed from the others to get their job done. Because they were buried in their specific tasks, they never looked up to see if the other links in the chain were

Communicating your perspective, while taking the time to understand and appreciate others, helps make collaboration possible.

holding, and they neglected their whole reason for being: the customer. To his credit, the waiter as conduit between the customer and kitchen took responsibility to get the order right, but he was only as successful as the kitchen staff behind him.

Effective collaboration means that *everyone* understands not just a shared goal, but also the different context in which each individual or team is operating. In our salad example, the customer's measure of success was a fresh salad, made to order, delivered quickly. The waiter wants to take and fulfill the customer's order quickly and create a positive experience so he or she gets a good tip. The kitchen staff needs to fulfill the order quickly, is probably reading off a standard recipe page, and focusing on the exact amounts of each ingredient to stay within budget. If each member of the team is operating in their own bubble and doesn't make it clear what success looks like and how it fits into the success of others, you end up with a botched salad. Communicating your perspective, while taking the time to understand and appreciate others, helps make collaboration possible.

In many companies, people in different departments take turns, either working or observing a day in the life of their counterparts. Even if your organization doesn't have this kind of formal program, spend some time with others with whom you work to get a sense of the pressures and challenges they face. Walking in someone else's shoes will help you collaborate more effectively.

Ask yourself:

- What do I need from others around me to be successful?

- What do others need from me to ensure their success?

- What are the obstacles that might make it difficult for others to help me?

- How do I ensure that I am communicating what I need from them, and conversely, that I can understand what they need from me?

Chapter 24

Beware the Word Monger

Several years ago, while working with a client, I found myself stuck in word-mongering hell. We were drafting an op-ed piece for a major metropolitan daily about an issue very much in the news. The client insisted that the draft of the article be reviewed by Marketing, HR, Legal and the Product Development team. Each group had edits, most of which had nothing to do with the actual content. They were suggesting minor changes, like replacing the word "use" with "util-ize." ("Utilize" sounds impressively authoritarian to the amateur, but journalists all over the world are trained from the first day to always use "use." So, changes like this put my teeth on edge. Just so you know.) The back-and-forth was maddening; a slow death by a thou-sand paper cuts. By the time we finished "editing" the op-ed piece, we had missed our window of opportunity. All that time and effort was wasted, and our voices not heard.

I call this *word mongering*, and it often is one of the biggest symptoms of poor collaboration. All too often this is called "wordsmithing," which refers to someone who has specific skill with words. Word mongering, on the other hand, is a nagging talent that uses the red pen to stop something from moving forward or to assert influence in the organization. Written documents, blog posts and reports become weapons in an ongoing power struggle within organizations. While giving various departments an opportunity to weigh in might be a good step toward collaboration, this over-editing does just the opposite.

When people spend hours and hours crossing out and rewriting, it isn't about grammar. It's often because they don't want to own a particular direction or point of view. The continuous updates offer a way to avoid dealing with the real issues that involve true intellectual wrestling over a position, opinion or strategic direction. Word mongering can also be a way to exert control, to make sure that the person doing the editing leaves their stamp. All of this defies the spirit of collaboration. Even if the true intent is to be helpful.

To be sure, editing and proofing written documents is crucial. The input of others who see the issue from different perspectives can amplify your point of view or prevent you from making a huge mistake. When editing is constructive, it can make a document better. When you find yourself on draft 14, changing "the" to "a," you're probably in trouble.

How do you avoid being a word-monger?

Check the change. Do the changes you are making correct inaccuracies or bad information? If not, think twice before you type.

Seek meaning. Ask yourself if the sentences you want to change are unclear or hard to understand. If so, change may be warranted. If the thought is clear, but just not the way you would say it, leave it alone.

Test vocabulary. Do you feel compelled to replace a simple word with an impressive one or just feel the need to add syllables? If the meaning is clear, resist. Big words don't make you look smarter. Follow the rule that most journalists use—would someone in the 10th grade understand this?

Examine intent. Use the *Prism of Value* to understand your intentions. Take a hard look at what the writer really wants to say and why. Are you, as a reviewer, contributing to making the writer successful? Are you enhancing the piece, clarifying the point of view or clouding it? Are you preventing the writer from presenting a biased or false argument or from inadvertently offending the intended audience? Are your comments enhancing the meaning?

Listen to the voice. Here's the tough part. Being a good editor means to listen to the voice—not in your head—but in the writer's head. Is the writer's voice effective as casual, conversational? Does it really need to be changed to sound business formal or legal, or is that merely your own personal style preference? Even if you think your word choice or phrasing might be more powerful or compelling, ask yourself if you are simply trying to make your mark.

> **Think twice before turning on "Track Changes" and understand your true motivation for making that change.**

Commit. Have something to contribute? Make the change and leave it alone. Nothing wastes more energy and angst than a back-and-forth, comment-by-comment set of blows over issues like whether to start a sentence with "and."

Know When to Fold. When you are getting ready to add your two cents to the document, stop and ask if your edits or suggestions are making the document better. Are you clarifying or simply trying to leave your stamp? If the thought is clear but just not the way you would say it, leave it alone and move on.

Power and dominance show up not just in board meetings, but in the back-and-forth of our written communication. Think twice before turning on "Track Changes" and understand your true motivation for making that change.

Ask yourself:

- In making comments to a document, am I making it better?

- Is the document clear as it is?

- What insights or comments could I provide that make the document better?

Chapter 25

Collaboration From Stalled to Successful

In 2009, 12 representatives from half a dozen nonprofit organizations around the nation's capital sat in a room prepared to do something momentous. Each of these organizations works on the front lines in neighborhoods where gang violence, drugs, high school dropout rates and low-wage jobs that barely cover rent and food are everyday realities. The six organizations support parents and children fighting for a better life through good education, job training, medical care, mental health services and other supports. That day, they were sitting around the table to explore ways to collaborate to make a bigger impact on the children and families in a neighborhood where they each worked.

What brought them together was Venture Philanthropy Partners (VPP), an innovative philanthropic organization that aligns resources and actions to strengthen nonprofits to serve more youth in Greater Washington. VPP had previously worked with each of the organizations – providing dollars and strategic assistance to help the organizations increase and strengthen their individual capacity. Its leader, Carol Thompson Cole, believed that if these organizations could collaborate to integrate the health, early childhood education, career and college prep, and youth services and support, their collective impact could be game changing.

The stakes were high. VPP was exploring the possibility of making a major multi-year, investment to fund a collaborative effort.

The leaders of these organizations all knew each other. They shared clients; they went to civic meetings to testify on key issues; and they participated in programs offered by common funders. Unfortunately, they also saw themselves as competitors for the same pot of resources. Despite their shared interests, they were careful with each other. Some had tried to work together in past but had not previously collaborated at the level required for this type of effort.

Here they were in the same room with a facilitator to explore whether there was any possibility that they could collaborate for a greater good. During the session, these executives had the opportunity to share their aspirations and frustrations. Gradually, they started to lower their guards. The two groups saw each other in a new light: Maybe they *could* be partners, not rivals.

When the time came for another meeting to push the effort forward, the group couldn't find a mutually convenient time when they could all talk again. The shared vision the group developed and the promise of more funding weren't enough to create that essential shift they all thought they wanted. They were stuck in the Prism of Me. In the aftermath of the 2008 recession, these organizations were struggling for funds. One day of meeting was neither enough to get beyond

their individual needs, nor eliminate the lack of trust they still har-
bored.

Undaunted, Carol and her team stepped back and thought hard
about why the effort failed. Three issues emerged:

- Lack of trust

- Lack of incentives (each organization wanted money for
  themselves, not just to be part of a shared effort)

- Inability of these organizations on their own to define the
  benefits of collaboration

Armed with this knowledge and insight, Carol and her team went
back to the drawing board. With a federal grant from the Social
Innovation Fund (SIF), VPP created youthCONNECT to bring
these six organizations together. In its first two years, the
youthCONNECT SIF Network served more than 10,000 people,
and by the time the SIF grant ended, the youthCONNECT partners
served more than 25,000 young people. The success of the collaboration caught the attention of Prince Georges County Executive
Rushern Baker, who brought the youthCONNECT network to
Suitland High School. The program morphed into *Ready to Work*,
attracting new partnerships with businesses and other philanthropic
organizations.

From a failed first attempt came some powerful lessons.

**Get the right people with the right balance of personalities at the
table.** People who are committed to working together can balance
their individual needs with those of a greater good. This means that
people must be willing to be honest about what they want and identify their shared interest and values.

Take the time and find the space to build trust. Collaboration is about sharing power and resources for a greater good. It's not enough to have a shared vision of that common interest. You must also have the belief that everyone will act in the interests of the collaboration, not just for themselves. There must be space and time for people to build trust by openly sharing their ambitions and their concerns. Don't expect immediate results. Create the environment and structure where people are able to have some difficult conversations. Enlist the help of a neutral facilitator to provide assistance. Remember that collaborative efforts take time. People must be committed to look at the effort through the *Prism of Value*, committed to what they can contribute to a joint effort, and what larger good the collaboration will bring.

Set expectations for outcomes. Each member of the group must be clear about the expectations and goals of the collaborative effort. For collaboration to happen, a group must be able to freely discuss rewards and risks and be in alignment about what they are. Without expectation-setting and alignment, collaborative efforts will fail.

Clarify roles to create collaborative tissue. Clearly articulating the roles, responsibilities and expectations of all participants from the beginning minimizes tension and accelerates the work. Establish a set of ground rules or guiding principles for behavior such as youthCONNECT's "Do No Harm" document.

Some of the best collaborative efforts can be found in hospital ERs and among first responders. Doctors, nurses, firefighters, police and EMS technicians who have never met often find themselves working together on a shift, under very high-stress circumstances. Hospital teams and first responders frequently hold simulations of mass-casualty incidents. By doing so, they forge trust. More importantly, they develop and reinforce clear patterns of behavior and action, creating a kind of organizational muscle memory. Everyone is able to spring into action quickly. Individually they know what to do, but they also know how to work with others and share information quickly.

Find or be the ringleader. In every group, there must be someone who takes the lead organizing the group and pushing it forward. There must be a structure that coordinates the convening, information-sharing and organization of the collaboration. VPP played that role in obtaining financial and other resources necessary to support the effort. But it was important that in providing those resources, VPP didn't dominate or dictate what the network should do. In smaller, less complex efforts, an individual or a small team could play that role. The important thing is that there has to be someone or something that drives the collaboration forward at the beginning and helps keep the momentum going throughout while ensuring that power remains with the group.

Balance individual and group needs. The group must decide what work must be done together, and when it makes sense for people go off and work individually. Everyone in the group needs to feel that they are making a unique and important contribution. They need to have their fingerprints individually on their portion of the responsibility. By doing so, the individuals become more invested with "skin in the game." By same token, the individuals need to do and share their work within the context of the group's objectives and purpose.

> **The challenge for each of us is to understand and believe that together our sum is greater than our parts.**

Develop a shared language. Everyone comes to a collaborative effort bringing their individual view of the world and their own way of communicating. Many times, common words like "goals", "strategy," "resources" and "accountability" mean different things to different people. It is important that everyone has a shared understanding of key terminology and concepts.

Communicate effectively. Underlying any collaborative effort is the need for effective communication. Information is power. Groups need to decide how often and in what ways they will share information. Each member of the group must be willing to provide information. Meetings are a form of communication as well, and members need to be present.

Respect. Understanding and celebrating what each person or organization in the group brings to the equation is essential. So is understanding and respecting the differences among the group.

Recognize that things will not always go smoothly. Even with the best planning and communication, there will be conflicts or unexpected events that throw an initiative off track. The relationships and trust you've built will sustain the effort.

Collaboration isn't easy. The challenge for each of us is to understand and believe that together our sum is greater than our parts. With that belief, we must then create the space and opportunity for collaboration and power-sharing to take place. Collaboration, like anything else worthwhile, is hard work, but when done well, the rewards are enormous.

Ask yourself:

- What can we do together that can't be achieved alone?

- What might the rewards be of us working together? What might we gain?

- What are the risks we might face working together? What might we lose?

- How do we have the conversations we need to have? Do we need a facilitator?

- Who is our ringleader and what is that person's role?

- Do we have the right people at the table to collaborate?

- Are we clear on why we are collaborating and what we want to achieve?

- What resources do we need to support a collaborative effort?

- Who or what is our backbone?

- How will we communicate with each other?

- How will we hold each other accountable?

- What do we hope to achieve and by when?

- How will we know what we have achieved?

- How will we manage conflict?

- How will we share credit?

Chapter 26

Be the Habit No One Wants to Break (or, Making a Meal of Consistency)

Whenever we visit Miami, my husband and I always make a point of going to Joe's Stone Crab. Of course, we have to order the legendary stone crabs with mustard, the hash browns extra crispy, and a slice of key lime pie. It's a must for us, and it seems that no matter what time of day we go, we always wait at least an hour (and on the weekends two or three). According to Joe's blog, some people actually go there for the wait itself, just to see and be seen.

Joe's offers great food and great service delivered by wait staff who are well trained and empowered to serve. In their black tuxedos, they communicate tradition, professionalism, efficiency, welcome and fun. The restaurant is a well-oiled machine that has been turning out wonderful meals for more than a century, grossing $38 million a year along the way. Joe's, like Southwest Airlines, Ikea, Starbucks and other longstanding brands, has created what former Proctor and Gamble Chairman A. G. Lafley and business professor Roger Martin call *cumulative advantage*—maintaining a consistency of brand experience that makes it easy and comfortable for customers to choose you. Joe's is a habit for Miami residents and tourists alike, a habit that you don't want to break once you're hooked. Just a few doors down, newer restaurants are half empty. Crowds flock to Joe's every day. It's also a habit for staff, who once hired, tend to stay. Some have been there for half a century.

Joe's success offers some powerful lessons whether you are trying to build your personal brand or that of your company and organization. It is a textbook example of Lafley's and Martin's four tenets of cumulative advantage.

Establish popularity early. Being first on the scene in customers' minds is something marketers have sought for years. When Joe Weiss and his wife opened their restaurant with a few tables on the front porch of their house in 1914, there weren't many places to eat in the area. They started serving stone crab, which was unique to Florida, and established Joe's as *the* place to get this Sunshine State crustacean treat.

As you are building your personal brand, think about what you offer within your organization that will make people want to work with you again and again, to request you on their teams. It could be as simple as delivering every project on time without drama or writing so well you make your team look good. If you are building an organizational brand, find ways to get your customers to choose you—a free trial, competitive pricing—to hook them on your product or service.

Design for habit. Make it easy for people to use your services and talents and don't leave it up to chance. Amazon does this brilliantly with its one-click and reordering options. It's so convenient, fast and simple to buy from them that it has become a habit, even if they aren't the lowest price. It's important that people see your offering in the context of their environment or situation.

Look at your business card. Will the recipient of your card remember you the next day and why they should call you? Is it easy to find the contact information? Look at your website. Is it easy to engage with you? Can interested visitors quickly sign up for your newsletter or blog? Your visual look or identity should make it easy for people to connect with you on an ongoing basis.

Innovate inside your brand. Joe's is known for stone crab, but the restaurant continually adds new things to the menu while keeping the staples. In fact, the menu is quite large. Twenty years ago, the restaurant partnered with a Chicago-based restaurant group, Lettuce Entertain You Enterprises, to bring Joe's to other markets. Together they opened Joe's Seafood, Prime Steak and Stone Crab in Chicago, and later in Las Vegas and Washington, DC. They also built an online ordering system so you could enjoy the taste of Joe's back home. But as they expanded and added new menu items, Joe's has been careful to maintain the cumulative advantage of the old.

Are you adding new services? Are you taking advantage of technology and communications platforms to deliver what you offer in fresh ways? For example, if you have a newsletter, have you considered creating some short videos to share your ideas? Are you developing new skills and staying ahead of trends in your industry?

Keep your communication simple. People are always looking for the line of least resistance. As discussed throughout this book, don't overly complicate your message. There is too much noise and competition for our attention. Experts say you have three seconds to make an impression. If people can't quickly grasp why they should use your product or service or engage with you, they will move on to someone else. Joe's message: a great meal and great service.

Practice cumulative communications. Joe's message and brand is amplified, not only by simple communication, but by cumulative communication—follow up, follow through and follow on. It's a continual reinforcement of what the brand is all about both internally and externally. Each experience builds on the previous one, with the eventual advantage of cumulative effect, which is more powerful than the isolated experiences.

Joe's continually reinforces its message of great meal and great service in words and in actions. The food is well prepared with excellent ingredients. Everyone, including servers, bar tenders and table captains, continually reinforces the message. It starts with great hiring. Our server told us she had to go through four interviews before she was hired. They train and then reinforce the training every day. On a busy Friday night, the affable manager,

> **Building staying power comes from being committed to who you are…through consistent actions and words that express your unique value.**

wearing a spectacular gray suit, chatted up customers and bussed tables when the wait staff got busy. With those actions, he was sending some powerful messages. One, serving the customer was paramount. Two, pitching in wherever staff is needed is expected and valued. Three, serving with a smile and sincere desire to make the diner feel good is expected and valued.

The lesson of Joe's is that it isn't enough to create a fan club. You want to be the habit no one wants to break. Building staying power comes from being committed to who you are and what you bring to the world and reminding people over and over again through consistent actions and words that express your unique value.

Ask yourself:

- What makes you a habit that your customers, clients, friends and family don't want to break?

- Are you reliable and accountable?

- What actions do you take every day that reaffirm and reinforce the experiences that your clients, customers, colleagues, friends and families can expect from you?

- How are you adding value by contributing something that makes life easier, safer, happier and healthier, or by reducing stress, frustration, danger, heartburn or heartache?

Chapter 27

Actions Really Do Speak Louder than Words

Whether building a career or a company, success comes from hard work, talent and the ability to stay the course. This last part is what derails most people. You've developed a brand position and you have a powerful message. Now comes the hard part: living out what and who you say you are, and delivering on that brand promise every day.

The Ritz Carlton hotels stand apart for their legendary customer service. Their motto is: "Ladies and Gentlemen Serving Ladies and Gentlemen." They don't just provide wonderful service. Their employees are encouraged to go one step further, to fulfill even the *unexpressed* wishes and needs of their guests.

While cleaning a room one day, a housekeeper noticed that the guest was reading *The Girl with the Dragon Tattoo*, the first in a trilogy of gruesome thrillers by Swedish writer Stig Larsson. At almost any other hotel brand, that casual observation would have been the end of the story. But because Ritz Carlton employees are focused on *anticipating* needs and wants, the housekeeper first cleaned the room, then went out to a bookstore and bought the other two books in the series. She left the books on the nightstand with a note that said she shared the guest's love for these books and thought the guest would enjoy reading the other two.

If the guest wasn't already a loyal Ritz Carlton guest, most likely she became one after that gesture. The housekeeper didn't see herself simply as the person cleaning room 836, but rather as an integral player in creating optimal guest experiences. Her role was to serve the guest, not simply make her bed. Ritz empowered her to buy those books (they give employees the authority to spend a certain amount of money to create great guest experiences) and in so doing, elevated the role of the housekeeper. That is what living your brand looks like.

Ritz Carlton, like other successful brands, practices *cumulative communications*—a reinforcement of its messaging and brand every day until it is so ingrained in employees and customers they can't help thinking of new ways to delight and impress. The housekeeper story is only one of

> **Cumulative communications give you cumulative advantage...**

hundreds of similar stories that have become company lore. The motto is repeated to employees continually, and they are encouraged to find their own way to deliver. Because this behavior is so integrated in the company culture, it won't fall apart when there is a change of leadership.

Cumulative communications give you cumulative advantage, where you are so irresistible you become a habit that others don't want to break. If you can *say* it, you can *be* it, and if you can be it, you can *live* it. Saying, being and living is a continuous cycle. Not only is it important to communicate messages, it is also important for organizations to celebrate and honor the behavior they seek to encourage.

Living your brand isn't just something done in the for-profit world. For instance, Aspire Public Charter Schools is a charter management organization based in California, with a mission to prepare K-12 students for success in college, career and life. Founded by Silicon Valley entrepreneur Reed Hastings and former Modesto county Superintendent of Schools Don Shalvey, Aspire has achieved what has been elusive for organizations with far more resources and marketing dollars. Starting with a few schools, the organization now consists of 40 schools serving 16,000 students in economically challenged communities in California and Tennessee. For the last eight years, every graduating student has been accepted at a four-year institution.

Aspire has been able to achieve this success by having a clear mission and message, not only with teachers and principals, but with custodians, cafeteria workers, parents and students. Like the Ritz, they have a simple motto: "College is for Certain."

One of the ways they reinforce it is by practicing UFOs—Unexpected Fortuitous Observations. It began one day when a principal overheard a custodian say to a student, "You look like you know how to walk on a college campus. Keep doing that, because that's how they walk at Cal Tech." The principal told Shalvey, who then sent an email to the custodian to thank him for helping to change the opportunity for the student. But it didn't stop there. The custodian's story was shared throughout Aspire. The custodian was celebrated like a rock star, which encouraged other custodians, cafeteria workers, parents and teachers to think of ways to interact with students and reinforce the message.

Shalvey believes that if you look at the unique contribution that all the adults in the school make, then you can develop cultural institutions that will support and nurture this behavior through ordinary action, repeated day in and day out.

The regular communication and reinforcement of the best of your brand is what makes it possible to deliver consistently. That commitment to saying and living your brand is what gives you staying power, and both *competitive* and *cumulative* advantage.

Ask yourself:

When looking at yourself and your organization, are you clearly articulating and acting on clear messages about yourself and your company or nonprofit?

- Do you view your daily interactions with family, friends, co-workers, customers and vendors through the Prism of Value, thinking about what you contribute to those relationships that's positive and how you can reduce or eliminate the negatives?

- How could you reinforce the positives you add and negatives you remove in your communications with those who matter to your success?

- Do you call out positive actions of others to reinforce what you believe are good practices and habits? Or do you only complain when others make a mistake or behave badly?

Chapter 28

Be Like a Pilot: Convey and Confirm

Although I've flown hundreds of thousands of miles, I am afraid to fly. I would much prefer to stay on the ground. On long-haul flights, there used to be an option on the audio channels that allowed passengers to listen to the pilot conversations with the control tower. When everyone else was sleeping, I was tuned in. It was fascinating to hear the way the pilots and control towers talked to each other

Pilot: "United 483. Request permission to climb to 37,000 feet."

Tower: "Roger United 483. Permission to climb to 37,000 feet."

Pilot. "Roger UA 483. Permission to climb to 37,000."

Aside from the sneak preview of when we were going to change altitude, these transmissions gave me some important communication insights.

First, pilots and the air traffic controllers use precise language; no fluff or extra words. Second, they continually ensure that the other party has heard, and understood, the intent of their communication.

They convey information, acknowledge that it was received, and then confirm understanding; in this case, permission to climb to a higher altitude. There are clear protocols to prevent misunderstandings. Without this kind of precision, there could be terrible crashes. In fact, a study by Airbus found that incorrect and incomplete communication between pilots and controllers was the cause of 80 percent of incidents or accidents.

How many "communication crashes" occur every day because we haven't made sure the other party has heard and understood what we were saying? You miss a deadline because you didn't fully understand what your boss was asking. You are late for an important client meeting because they gave you the wrong address. A painting crew paints the wrong office, leading to a five-figure loss. Or worse, a surgeon removes the healthy lung from a patient, leaving the diseased one behind.

Just because you sent an email or had a quick conversation with someone doesn't mean the recipient truly heard you...

Just because you sent an email or had a quick conversation with someone doesn't mean the recipient truly heard you the way you intended or that they plan to do what you ask. How often do our emails, phone calls, and texts go unanswered, leaving us to wonder: Did they receive my message, or is it lost in the ether? Did the recipient understand my message? Are they angry? Are they going to respond? Are they just overwhelmed? To be sure, our electronic inboxes are inundated, but not responding sends a message that you don't care or that you're just rude.

I was reminded of this when someone emailed me asking if I was going to attend a conference, and if so, would we want to travel together to save on expenses? I wasn't sure I could go, and instead of simply replying that I hadn't decided, I didn't reply at all, leaving that person to think that I had "ghosted her" and that I wasn't interested in our professional friendship. Nothing could have been further from the truth.

Clarity of communication is critical, especially when communicating by email or text. If you are asking someone to do something, be clear about *what* the task is, *when* you need it done, and most importantly, *why* you need it done. You can avoid wasting time and energy by answering those basic questions.

If you are receiving that email, let the recipient know you got it, understood it, and when you are going to get back to them. If you're busy, how long does it take to say, "Got it, but can't respond just now." Those simple words show respect because you are communicating that you heard them. If you are going to be unavailable for a period of time, let people know so they have appropriate expectations for when you will respond, or, if you are away on vacation, they know to get the task done through another person.

By the same token, just because someone doesn't respond to you doesn't mean that they are rude. They may just be busy or sick. Their lack of response, however, does not mean you are off the hook. Let's say your boss asks you to write part of a proposal. You aren't sure what she has in mind, so you email her back and get silence for two days. Email again but express some urgency, or better yet, pick up the phone or walk down the hall and see if you can get two minutes of her time to get the information you need. Communication is not a passive act. Both sides of the conversation have a responsibility to ensure that the other hears and understands. As a recipient of communication, you must listen both to the words and the *intent* behind the words, and if you don't understand, make the effort to get what you need.

One caveat—don't get carried away. Once it's clear that both parties understand the communication, don't get caught up in the email volley that can descend into an emoji boomerang and wasted time.

"Got it. Will have it tomorrow."

"Good."

"Glad you are happy."

"Thanks."

Communication involves a commitment to ensure that you understand and are understood. Thinking a bit more like airline pilots and controllers offers a good model for taking the time to confirm what's conveyed.

Ask yourself:

- Have you just sent it and forgotten it, or are you making follow-up a part of your communication?

- In what ways might you make it easier for people to respond to your requests for help and information?

- Are you responding to emails and other communication when others need something from you?

- What practices can you put in place for yourself to ensure that you aren't sending and forgetting?

- How might you better structure your emails or other communication to get the responses you seek?

Chapter 29

Conflict Happens

Early in my communications and public relations career, I hired Debbie Disasteras. A good friend and colleague recommended her highly. Debbie had done an internship at a world-class newspaper, had great writing samples, and seemed to have a good work ethic, which my friend confirmed. None of it turned out to be true. Her writing was dull and ponderous; the samples had all been heavily edited. She showed up late for work every day and complained when we needed her to stay late to meet a deadline. She couldn't work independently, and she needed lots of handholding, which was at odds with a fast-paced, get-it-done atmosphere.

I was angry with my friend for misleading me. I was angry with Debbie for not being who she said she was. And I was angry with myself for not making a better hiring decision. So, I did what any smart manager would do. Nothing. I didn't want to have the tough conversation with my friend about how I resented her for recommending Debbie, and I didn't want to confront Debbie about her performance issues. The situation just got worse.

Other team members were frustrated by Debbie's incompetence, and it began to create an uncomfortable environment for everyone. Debbie made veiled threats to sue us for creating a hostile workplace. She eventually got another job and the situation resolved itself, but I can't credit my leadership or my communication. I avoided the conflict at every opportunity.

Face it. Conflict happens. It's not a question of *if*, but *when*, and in what form. Conflict happens when what we want, need or expect doesn't align with what others want, need or expect. It happens because we want to control or because we feel threatened. When this misalignment occurs, how we communicate can make the difference between resolution or dissolution of relationships, business dealings or opportunities for promotion.

In my experience, there are four *personas* that take over when a conflict occurs:

Dominators have to be in charge. They like to be right and win no matter what. It's their way or the highway. This can be effective during a crisis or when there is an urgent situation that must be resolved quickly. These folks take charge, make decisions and tell others what to do. But dominators don't like dissent, and this approach can quash valuable feedback from others. Many dominators scream, yell and bully. This helps dissipate their anger or anxiety but can leave ugly scars for those around them.

Avoiders do everything in their power not to deal with a conflict at all. They deny, ignore and hope, as I did, that a problem will go away, even as it remains unresolved or worse, festers. Some-times these people show their aggression in a passive way. They don't return your calls, or if you ask them to perform a task they don't want to do, they do it poorly so you won't ask again. This is the assistant who puts 20 sugars in the coffee you asked him to make, then feigns surprise when you complain, telling you, "That's how I learned to make coffee," when what he *really* wanted to tell you was that he was insulted you asked him in the first place.

Peacemakers will do whatever it takes to avoid drama. They acquiesce and accommodate others for the sake of tranquility. They *believe* they're demonstrating cooperation and flexibility, but if they give in too much, they're perceived as weak. They may feel resentful but they would never let on because they don't want to make a fuss. So, they don't.

Collaborators face the conflict and work with others to resolve it. They seek middle ground, willingly giving up something they value to get a mutually agreeable situation. They seek to understand and be understood. They will work to see the other side and understand that for them to win, others must win as well.

When you find yourself in a difficult situation, you must find a way to step back to understand what's really happening. If you understand the emotional triggers that drive your colleagues, clients and customers, you are in a better position to defuse and manage conflicts.

> **If you understand the emotional triggers…you are in a better position to defuse and manage conflicts.**

What matters to the people who matter most to you will influence your relationship and your success. Tensions rise when whatever is most treasured—whether it's power, reputation, image, wealth, ease or simplicity—is in jeopardy. When that happens, people slip into their *conflict persona*.

In the next few chapters, we'll discuss how to recognize *emotional triggers* and *conflict personas* and find ways to communicate more effectively when under pressure and under fire – and get what you want.

Ask yourself:

- What is your conflict persona?

- How does that show up at home and in your workplace?

- What is the conflict persona of your boss, your spouse or your client?

Chapter 30

That's Not What I Meant

Carl was Executive Vice President of Communications at a large national trade association. Kathy was Carl's deputy and oversaw the organization's media relations. Kathy was as good as they get, garnering major feature articles in *The New York Times* and *The Wall Street Journal*. She even had the CEO appear on *The Today Show*. These news outlets are the Holy Grail for public relations people. When it came time for performance reviews, Carl recommended that Kathy get a seven percent raise—three percent *more* than the average for association staff—and a promotion to the next pay level.

The money was great, but what Kathy *really* wanted was a title change, from Communications Manager to VP of Communications, to reflect her actual role. Carl told her that wasn't possible given the organization's title protocols, and then he congratulated her on her great performance. Kathy asked if Carl could go to HR and ask for an exception. Carl declined, telling her what really mattered was the money. Furious, Kathy stormed out of Carl's office and told the rest of the team how insensitive he was. Carl was flabbergasted. He had just given Kathy the biggest percentage raise in the history of the organization and she was angry? Talk about misalignment.

Both Carl and Kathy had the same set of facts: great performance, a healthy raise. Carl's *intention* was to show Kathy how much the organization valued her work by giving her such a big raise. For him, *money* was a sign of esteem and success. Kathy perceived the raise as an empty gesture. Money didn't hold the same emotional value to her that it did to Carl. Her parents gave her money whenever she wanted it but never spent much time with her. Her motivation was fueled by the desire for *attention*.

What she wanted was respect, notice and public recognition. No one else would ever know just how successful she was without the change in title. Carl was now angry because Kathy was badmouthing him to the rest of team. He had given Kathy a *gift*, and she didn't appreciate him or the raise. Carl and Kathy never bothered to understand each other's perceptions and intentions. They barely spoke, and within a few months, Kathy left the company.

Political strategist and pollster Frank Luntz says communication isn't so much about what you say, but what people hear. Whether true or not, others' perception of you is their reality.

Like Carl, you may have good intentions, but those intentions might get lost in translation. People process information and actions through the lens of their experiences and emotions.

Had either Carl or Kathy used their Prism of Value to understand the other's frustrations, each might have understood the other's frustrations.

They might have better been able to communicate, and the organization might still have Kathy on the team.

What could Carl and Kathy have done differently?

Listen carefully. They could have removed their respective filters and listened to each other with the sincere desire to understand someone else's perspective. In this case, Carl was praising her and giving her something *he* thought was affirming, even if it wasn't what she wanted. This could have been a great opportunity for Carl to enrich his understanding of how Kathy is best motivated – and how to retain her.

Acknowledge what the speaker said. In this case, Kathy could have thanked Carl for the raise, showing that she understood what he was trying to do for her. By doing so, she would have given Carl positive reinforcement for his action, which would likely have made him more open to hearing her point about the title.

Observe reactions. Had Carl been paying attention, he might have noticed that Kathy didn't smile and seemed very subdued in the face of good news.

Ask clarifying, non-judgmental questions. Had Carl taken note of Kathy's subdued reaction, he might have asked, "How are you feeling about this?" A more open-ended question demonstrates his empathy and sincere caring. A statement like, "Wow, you seem unhappy" might have put Kathy on the defensive. By asking Kathy how she's *feeling* about the raise, he's opening the door for Kathy to say, "I appreciate the raise, but I was hoping for a title change as well. Because when I go outside the organization, people tend to perceive my role as more junior."

Restate what you hear. Carl could then have said, "I understand how frustrating the title may be for you." In this way, Kathy feels that Carl gets her and isn't dismissing her concerns.

Clarify your intentions. After acknowledging what he heard from Kathy, Carl might have then said, "Kathy, your work has been outstanding. I wanted to show you how much we appreciate you by giving you a substantial raise. I know how important a title change is, and I am not able to do anything about that right now because of our strict title protocols. My hands are tied on this one." Here he has reaffirmed his intention to praise Kathy through monetary reward and explained why he can't make a title change.

The intention-perception gap often is at the root of most conflicts. We often assume the worst. As a boss, you think you are providing constructive criticism, while your staff member thinks you just yelled at him. Like Carl, you think you are being a positive, engaging leader, but your employee feels that your actions aren't good enough. Taking the time to understand what someone else is feeling and thinking is essential to closing the gap between what you intend and how someone else interprets it.

> **The intention-perception gap often is at the root of most conflicts.**

Statements and Questions to Understand Intentions and Perceptions

- It sounds like what you're saying is…

- It sounds like what is most important to you is…

- I'm not sure I quite understand…

- What I heard you say is… did I hear you right?

- Can you say a little more about that?

- You've shared a lot of information, let me see if I've gotten this right…

- So, it seems like what you're telling me is, with this raise, you might be feeling both disappointed that you didn't get the title and appreciative of the money, all at the same time?

- I get the sense that you might be feeling…

- I think I've heard a few things that are important to you… first… second… third…

- Let me sum up what I think I've heard…

- Let's brainstorm additional ways that we can work on… that will be meaningful to you.

Chapter 31

Managing Conflict (or, Don't Become Anyone's Raw Meat)

An association asked me to facilitate their board of directors' retreat. The group had undergone a branding and positioning process, and when they rolled it out to their membership, the reaction was fierce, swift and negative. The members, many of whom had been involved with the organization for decades, hated the change and were shocked and surprised that such a major decision had been made in secret without involving the membership. In the end, the issue wasn't so much about the new name or logo. It was the way the change rolled out. The damage had been done and the incident exposed a number of rifts between the board and the membership.

Fingers pointed. Insults were hurled. It was a mess. At their upcoming board meeting, the first since the debacle, the organizers wanted to accomplish two things: have a good and healthy discussion of what happened so they could move forward, and then agree on a strategic direction.

As I always do, I had prepared thoroughly, reading through business and marketing plans, reviewing organizational history, and combing the website. I interviewed key board members to understand their thoughts and feelings about the incident and their ideas for the organization's future. I designed a detailed agenda. Finally, I arrived a day early to have dinner with the board and get to know the key players. A recipe for success, I thought. Not exactly.

The part of the retreat that dealt with the conflict went smoothly. I had asked the participants to write on large sticky notes how they felt about the incident and what they had learned. The questions were focused not on assigning blame, but rather on what lessons they could apply to future endeavors. They posted their thoughts on a wall and then, as a group, they looked at what each had written. Seeing emotions and thoughts on the wall acted as a kind of catharsis and stimulated a positive discussion. This retreat was going to be a home run, I thought. By the end of the day, I would be wrong.

After lunch, we started on the strategic planning part of the retreat. Every exercise I planned met resistance. The participants kept asking, "Why are we doing this?" I responded with what I thought were clear answers. The group didn't want to hear them. Rather than develop a strategic vision, they wanted to talk about specific tasks for the coming year. The more I pushed forward, the more they resisted. Sensing that I was losing control, the participants turned up the heat of their anger and frustrations. I had become raw meat and they pounced. I was dejected.

An essential part of communicating during conflict is understanding what is at the root of the conflict. Naming the proverbial elephant in the room can be scary, but it's necessary to unblock resistance. Afterword, I realized that what I *should* have done is stopped the retreat and talked about what I was noticing—their resistance—and then engaged the participants in a conversation about that.

When people are convinced that their way is the right way, it's difficult to resolve issues. When that happens, you may feel threatened, fearful and unsure, especially when you feel that you are solely responsible for the quality of the outcome of the project or challenge.

Here are a few tips to manage conflict where you're the one on the hot seat:

Keep calm and carry on. In 1939, these words appeared on a British motivational poster to keep morale high as the country was preparing for war. In recent years, the phrase has been adopted by commercial ventures. When facing down a surly employee or an angry client, the most important thing is to keep your emotions in check. If your emotions overtake you, you can't think or act clearly.

Don't react immediately. Unless someone is making a serious verbal or physical threat, don't react. Just listen. Let them vent. Often their frustration has built up over time. They need to express those concerns and experience that they are being heard. It doesn't mean you honor all their requests. It means that you *listen* and *acknowledge* what they have said.

Buy time. If the other person is screaming and yelling, or out of control, and gets angrier and angrier as they're talking, politely extricate yourself from the situation. Calmly say, "I can see you are very upset. Let's take a break and talk about this later." If they insist on continuing the tirade, simply say, "I don't do well when people yell, so I need to take a break. I'd be happy to come back later to discuss this." In this way you are taking the responsibility for the break. You are not judging and you're allowing the yeller to save face. The break gives you and the other person some time to calm down and reflect.

Avoid getting defensive. When you are having a conversation, try to listen objectively to the disagreement. Maybe they have point. Maybe your work *has* been lackluster, or the investor might be rightly frustrated that profits have been down for the past three quarters. Instead of launching a vigorous defense, note that you understand their frustration. Ask some clarifying questions, such as: "Where do you think I missed the mark on the proposal?" Acknowledge what they're telling you: "Yes, we're just as disappointed as you are that profits have been down."

Think forward. Don't get mired in assigning or accepting blame for something that has gone wrong. If you've made a mistake, say so. If you have caused harm, apologize. The trick is then to move on to what you are doing to fix it, and more importantly, prevent it from happening again. "Yes, profits have been down because our costs for labor and materials have increased sharply. In the coming months, we plan to…." Or, "I should have been more careful to catch spelling errors in the proposal. I have asked my co-worker to read over my copy before I send it on to you."

Stand tall in the face of conflict. Often there will be a team member or executive who is relentless in their criticism. Everyone else will be quiet and all eyes are on you. This is where they are silently deciding which side to take. Human nature being what it is, they will side with the stronger party. This is where you have to take a deep breath, swallow your anxiety and self-doubt, and have courage to stand by your thoughts and proposals. If others see your distress, they may push further, so watch your body language and don't slouch.

Harvard Business School professor and psychologist Amy Cuddy notes that when animals are threatened or seek dominance, they make themselves bigger. Think of a cobra ready to strike or the peacock displaying his feathers. Better yet, think of your favorite super hero. Have you ever seen Superman or Wonder Woman slouch? They stand firm when attacked. Cuddy suggests practicing power poses before meetings. Stand with both feet on the ground and hands on your hips. Although other psychologists haven't been able to replicate her results, I have found practicing this pose prior to a big presentation or an important meeting can help shift attention away from your own nerves and give you the appearance of confidence, even if that isn't what you are feeling inside.

Adopt "neutral face." Often in a meeting, we get distracted and start thinking about how we might be late to pick up the kids or what to do about dinner. Our facial expressions might

> **The key to managing conflict is to stay in control of your emotions and perspectives.**

change with our thoughts. Your colleague might say something that you disagree with, and your feelings appear all over your face. As this happens, we may unwittingly look hostile to someone else across the table. They don't know what we are thinking. It's important that we learn to adopt a neutral face so that we aren't sending messages we don't intend. Looking at your expressions in front of a mirror can help you see what you look like when you are happy, angry or sad. As you look at your different expressions, take a moment to examine what each expression *feels* like. When you find your neutral face, practice it and identify what kinds of thoughts help you create a calm, impartial demeanor. I'll never forget a high-powered woman telling me to look like I am on a Sunday afternoon walk when things get tough. It does work.

The key to managing conflict is to stay in control of your emotions and perspectives. Don't be anyone else's raw meat, letting others consume your views or even your identity. You can stand firm against someone trying to steamroll you or tell you who you are while remaining open to other points of view.

Ask yourself:

- How do you react when confronted by others?

- How might you calm yourself down to think more clearly about what is happening?

- How might you prepare for resistance to your ideas and proposals?

Chapter 32

On the Spot? Reframe, Redirect and Bridge

Turn on any newscast and you will have an opportunity to learn how to deal with conflict. Nothing feels more pressure-filled than being interviewed by a reporter on live television. There aren't opportunities for do-overs, and what you say and how you look will be on view for millions. Seasoned politicians and corporate executives invest heavily in media training so they can deliver their messages clearly. Their calm, unflappable demeanor comes after intensive preparation and practice. Those clever quips and comebacks are carefully crafted in advance so they can be rolled off the tongue at just the right time.

During the 1988 vice presidential debate between Senators Dan Quayle and Lloyd Bentsen, the latter delivered a devastating sound bite. Bentsen was nervous about the debate. He was not telegenic and the much younger Quayle was good on TV. In fact, Bentsen wanted to call the whole thing off. Instead, he and his team started to prepare. They knew that Quayle, in defending against his relative youth, habitually compared himself to President Jack Kennedy. Bentsen was ready. When Quayle started to talk about Jack Kennedy, Bentsen quickly shot back, "I knew Jack Kennedy. Jack Kennedy was a friend of mine. Senator, you're no Jack Kennedy." With that remark, Bentsen won the debate and created a sound bite heard round the world.

What he had done with that simple sound bite was *reframe* the conversation. By understanding some basic tenets of dealing with the media, you can learn how to manage hot situations on the fly.

Don't Repeat a Negative – Reframe it.

A PR colleague once told me a great story about how he reframed a tough question during a media interview. The reporter asked if the PR guy trained corporate executives to lie. His answer was, "No. I teach them how to tell the truth." When asked a negative question, most people repeat the falsehood to deny it, as in, "No, I don't teach people how to lie." The problem is that when you *repeat* the negative frame, you *reinforce* it. Let's take another example. Say

By understanding some basic tenets of dealing with the media, you can learn how to manage hot situations on the fly.

you are late for a meeting and your boss says, "Well, Ms. Smith, you're late once again." Instead of saying, "I'm sorry I'm late," you might frame it as, "There has been a problem on my bus route. I will have to find a better way to get to work." With this reply, you acknowledge the concern but redirect attention away from a transgression onto positive action you'll take to correct the problem. And you'd better find that speedier bus route.

Answering the Difficult Question

Every day we are asked questions we don't want to or perhaps cannot answer. Colleagues may ask you about strategy or personnel moves you might be planning to make but aren't ready to announce. Your boss may ask you for information you don't have and can't get. Just because a question is asked does not mean you have to answer it. One of the best ways to tell people that you don't want to comment or talk about something is simply to say, "I don't have any information or an opinion on that I can share right now. When I do, I'll let you know." Then go back to what you want to talk about. Let's say you were up for a promotion and you didn't get it. Dianne in Purchasing sees you in the break room and says," Gosh, you must be disappointed. What happened with that promotion?" Your answer might be to smile and say, "You win some and you lose some." One caveat. If your boss is asking about where a report is, you better answer it. If, however, she asks you about your sick father and you don't really want to get into it, simply say, "Doing as well as can be expected. Thanks for asking."

Bridges are Your Friend

Another way you can deal with difficult questions is to use the question as a bridge to what you can and do want to talk about. Let's say you are making a presentation to the Management Committee about your research on venues for your company's annual meeting. In the middle of your presentation, the COO asks you what you think about the cost-cutting measure that the company is implementing. You weren't expecting that question, and you don't want to answer because you disagree with the plan. You could say, "That's a great question because one of the factors we looked at in venue selection was cost. Let me share with you our recommendations." In this way you've acknowledged the question and can use it to find a way back to what you really want to talk about.

Deferring Your Response

There is a joke in the PR business:

Journalist: "How many PR folks does it take to change a light bulb?"

PR Person: "I don't know, but I'll get back to you."

Don't be afraid to say you don't know something. Nothing is worse than making something up or lying. In the end, lies tend to be revealed, and as they say, the cover-up is often worse than the original deed. If you are in a situation where you should know something but don't, acknowledge that and then tell the person you will get the answer for them. In the case of the COO pressing you for your thoughts on the new cost-cutting policy, you could say that you haven't fully processed its implications and would like to get back to her on that. Then you could say, "It's an important question, what are you hearing from others?"

Buy Time

When asked a tough question or one that you weren't prepared for, try to maintain a neutral demeanor. If you feel off-balance, take a breath and say something like, "That's an interesting question." You can also ask someone to repeat of the question, or you can ask another one: "I am curious, why do you ask?" All of these efforts give you some time to think about your response.

Avoid Hemming and Hawing

One of the most difficult things to do when faced with hostile or difficult questions is to hold your ground and not get rattled. Look your questioner in the eye (if you are uncomfortable doing so, look at their eyebrows or forehead), and pause and frame your response. Avoid looking up or downward or using lots of ums and ahs. This will project a lack of confidence or may be read as shiftiness.

Ask yourself:

- Can you identify some of these tactics when watching executives or politicians respond to tough questions from reporters?

- How effective are these spokespeople in communicating their message under pressure?

- What do you remember most from what they are saying?

- What are some tough situations you face? How might you use these tactics to better communicate?

- What are some ways you could tell someone you don't want to answer their question without saying that directly?

Afterward

Find Your Prism of Value

On a glorious spring day, I stopped by the cemetery where my brother Dave is buried. As I looked at the simple marker on his grave, I got a lump in my throat and a throbbing behind my eyes from tears that wanted to come but didn't. The words on the white marble summed up who Dave was—a loving son, brother and uncle. In the end, our lives are about the relationships we have with others and the legacy of those relationships. It's not about what we say when we are in the room but what others say and remember about us when we aren't there.

Among the many things I remember about Dave is his desire to connect with others. I hang onto the book he gave me on business strategy, even though it's too academic for me. The book reminds me of how Dave wanted to share something that mattered to him that he thought would be valuable to me. He wanted to contribute to the success of my business by offering something that he found useful.

But it is Dave's safe deposit box that is his legacy. Finding that he had put greeting cards, letters and photos from others who meant something to him in his safe deposit box gave me a whole new appreciation of the importance of communicating through a Prism of Value. When we frame what we want and have to offer through the lens of how we add positives to and subtract negatives from the lives of others, we are communicating our own value and meaning.

Effective communication really isn't about our words. It's about the positive experiences and feelings we engender among those we most want to connect with, convince and influence. Don't get me wrong. Words do matter. However, they are meaningless if they only speak to empty promises and unfulfilled action.

What matters most is our ability to forge relationships, and effective communication helps us do just that. As you move through the coming months and years, it is my hope that the lessons in this book will help you connect, convince and influence, bringing you success personally and professionally.

About the Author

Liz Wainger is a communications advisor, writer and speaker who has spent more than two decades showing executives and their teams how to frame and deliver messages that win hearts, minds and business. She is the founder of a strategic communications firm, Wainger Group, where she has developed campaigns, strategies and coaching workshops for Fortune 500 companies, start-ups, nonprofits and government agencies that inspire action and achieve results.

25470074R00109

Made in the USA
Columbia, SC
04 September 2018